THIS YEAR WILL BE DIFFERENT

© 2015, Monika Kanokova | www.mkanokova.com

Editor:	Monika Kanokova
	monikakanokova@gmail.com
Copy Editor:	Diana J. Joiner
	djjoiner925@gmail.com
Illustrator:	Ewelina Dymek
	ewelinadmk@gmail.com
Art Director:	Diana Ovezea
	type.design@me.com

Should you be holding a copy of this book you did not pay for, be an awesome human and make a donation to a local animal shelter. Be sure to mention your love for our book on Twitter or Instagram.

A CIP catalogue record for this book is available from the National Library in Austria.

ISBN 978-3-9503967-1-3

Monika Kanokova

The insightful guide
to becoming a freelancer

THIS YEAR
WILL BE
DIFFERENT

The fascinating freelance stories
of 23 successful women.

Contents

Introduction

Becoming self-employed is a big step, especially when you don't really know how to approach becoming so. Maybe you have already started building your own business, or maybe you're debating on whether you should take the jump to explore how it is to live as a freelancer. It all just seems a little risky, right?

Rumor has it that you must have at least six months worth of salaries saved before you even consider quitting your day job. I, however, found myself in a situation where my bank account was nowhere close to that number. I knew I'd have to make freelancing work from day one.

I read a great deal of books and challenged myself to learn about topics, such as invoicing, negotiating, time management, and strategies to build a passive income stream. All I knew was that I wanted to build a business I felt passionate to work for. The question then was, what would I have to do to actually pull it off?

I figured the best way for me to understand how to start my own business was to ask women I truly admire to share their stories with me.

I wanted to know how a writer makes money or how a translator can work from anywhere in the world. I wanted to know what it took to be a photographer and I wanted to understand how a travel blogger gets paid for traveling. I wanted to know a logical budget one needs to open a store and I wanted to get behind the scenes to learn how a fashion designer makes money. But most of all, I wanted to know how long it took them to run a business they could actually live off of comfortably.

I was deeply fascinated and touched by the honesty of all the stories these women shared with me. I felt inspired and encouraged by their learnings and became convinced that if I am fully focused and work hard, I would eventually be able to turn my dream job into a reality.

I should warn you, none of the women I interviewed said it was an easy battle. They all had their fair share of struggles or made some mistakes one way or another. They most certainly didn't have it all figured out right from the beginning as one may assume. As one woman, Maxie, said to me, "You don't have to be a born entrepreneur. No one is. It's a skill you can learn just like any other."

While hearing these stories, I knew that it was time for me to make my long-term dream come true and finally publish a book: the book you're currently holding in your hands.

In the following chapters, I will introduce you to 23 women who shared their stories with me, and now with you, on how they are achieving their goals and building their own unique businesses. I will go on to explain how to present yourself online, what the possibilities are to transition your hobby into a full-time career, and I'll give you a closer look at different resources that can help you build a business or make your existing business flourish even more.

I hope you enjoy reading the following pages as much as I enjoyed writing them; all of them were written with a big smile on my face. I hope you'll have the same smile on yours when you imagine yourself doing what you love and earning money in the process.

Let your new year be great, make it different, and start it today!
Love,
Monika

This book is dedicated to Janne van Dam who nudged me years ago to write a book, as well as Priscilla Osredkar who helped me get one of my first clients and whose paycheck was used to make this book a reality.

This project wouldn't have been possible without the great help of Diana Ovezea, Ewelina Dymek, and Diana J. Joiner, all of whom I found on Facebook, Behance, and Elance.

Put yourself on the map

The decision has been made: you're starting your own business! Congratulations!

Did you have someone applaud you when you told them you recently quit your job or that you want to build your own company? It happened to me, and right away, I was learning something from seeing those reactions. If you believe taking a particular path is the right decision for you, people will support it.

The first person who must believe that you can be your own boss is yourself. If you don't believe that you have what it takes to run your own shop, no one else will either. It might be that you need a certain something to make you grasp the realization that what you're about to do is authentic. It might also be that you're aware of who you are and what you want to do, but you don't have the guts to tell people just yet.

The truth is, you can be whatever you want to be in life, but for others to be able to recognize what you do and what they could hire you for, you must be open about your passions and services that you offer.

You might be still working in a café or perhaps you're pursuing a career, but you don't see yourself there for much longer. You can get out of where you are now and get to where you want to be next only if you share your vision and your dreams with people you're surrounded by.

Let's take a closer look at Oren's story because before she got her first assignment as an interior designer for a new restaurant, she spent ten months talking to people and left her business cards with everyone who crossed her path. ◆

11

Oren Lasry

INTERIOR DESIGNER, TEL AVIV

She refused to work for anyone else but herself. Oren got herself business cards, told everyone she met she was an interior designer, and kept doing so until someone hired her for a project. That was the start of her freelance career! In her interview, she speaks about the importance of giving back to the community and working not just "in" your business, but "on" your business.

What did you study and why?
I studied interior design at the Holon Institute of Technology. I wanted to become an event planner and producer and felt confronted by all the questions I had about space and spatial design. I planned to study business management afterwards, but during my studies I fell in love with creating interiors. I had found my passion.

13

What happened between your university diploma and your current career?
Straight out of university, I took on a handful of projects together with a friend. While this cemented my determination to succeed in this business, I didn't want to feel like I was compromising any part of my vision, so I decided to set up my own independent studio to specialize in commercial spaces.

What made you decide to become self-employed immediately after graduation?
I've always been a very independent person. I couldn't imagine sitting in a grey office every day from nine until nine, designing and drawing blueprints in someone else's name.

I went to a couple of job interviews, but because I never was that interested to become established in any of these companies, it didn't work out, which was probably for the better. Instead, I decided to look for my own projects. I have been self-employed for about two and a half years now.

What were the first steps to start your own business?
I printed myself business cards and brought them with me everywhere I went. I said I was an interior designer and asked people if they knew of any interesting projects I could get involved with. I was constantly out meeting and talking to people. This was before I even knew the value of networking and how to do it right. Today, I'm much more organized and I understand the value of networking effectively.

Back then, I also had two jobs to make some sort of a living. I worked in a gallery, which I thought would help me connect with the right audience, and I also worked in a bar, which was very a valuable time as it shed a lot of light on what to consider when I would later design nightlife spots.

14

It took me about ten months until a friend of mine called me and said she had a project and asked if I was interested. I got to design a Mexican restaurant, which turned into a chain, and I then designed all of the preceding restaurants. That's how everything started.

What were your first steps to create a successful business?
I've never worked in an architectural office, so everything I do is self-taught. I have developed a system that is my own and works for me and, most importantly, is best suited to meet my clients' needs.

> I've learned to understand that you need to spend about half of your time building your business instead of spending all of your time working on projects.

After about six months, I got myself some marketing help. I hired a marketing consultant who could tell me how to best and most effectively position my business. I needed to learn how to use Facebook, Pinterest, and all the other platforms, and also how to treat my former clients so they would keep me in mind and then refer me to their friends and acquaintances.

I've learned to understand that you need to spend about half of your time building your business instead of spending all of your time working on projects. It's often challenging because you're busy working on projects and don't have time to do anything else, but if you want to expand your business, you must become more attractive as a company. You must work 'on' your business and not just 'in' your business no matter what!

How do you work "on" your business?

I believe that creating the right kind of spaces can help add value to people's lives. Recently, I designed a new kindergarten concept, but not because I was getting paid for it. I noticed this area was under-developed, so I spent months researching several educational approaches. I prepared a detailed presentation and started pitching it to the municipality here in Tel Aviv. It was a lot of work with no remuneration in return, but they really liked it and now we've been receiving a budget. There are over 450 kindergarten classes administered by the Tel Aviv municipality and if the pilot proves to be successful, we could launch it on a national level. That might then be mutually beneficial for the children and teachers of the city.

I'm also teaching at The College Of Management to give back to the community. In general, I do my job not just because it pays the rent, but I believe I can improve people's lives. I often start working on projects because they're in a direction where I want to evolve.

How do you calculate your remuneration?

Usually, in architecture, it's common to take a certain percentage of the overall costs of the project. I believe that just because someone doesn't have much of a budget doesn't mean I will work less on their project than I would on one with enough money. I always try to estimate how much time I need for a project and explain to the client what I'll do during these days. I know what an hour of my time is worth, but I give discounts based on the size of the project.

I still don't earn what I feel would correlate to my efforts, but I can only get there if I continue working as I do at the moment. In the beginning, when you don't have much experience to prove you can actually achieve something, people might not trust you, so it's better to do projects for less and gain the work experience in return. If possible, don't work for free.

How big is your team?

It depends on the amount of projects I'm working on. Sometimes I work with two other freelancers, sometimes with one, and sometimes it's just me plus my expert handymen for things like wood, marble, air conditioning, iron, etc. I really believe in teamwork and I always try to involve as many people as possible. I like to work with a graphic and a product designer. It gives me a new perspective on the process and I learn a lot while working with people that possess different skills.

16

Usually, before I start working on a project, I estimate how many professionals I need to involve to get the best possible outcome.

How do you represent yourself online and what platforms do you consider important?

I've been using my Facebook as a business page since I started. I am now building my own website because although no one will hire you based solely on your profile, eventually they'll probably end up googling you. It's crucial that when they do, they find a strong, credible site: one that represents your business in the best possible light.

I often start working on projects because they're in a direction in which I want to evolve.

I also use Instagram and Pinterest to show design ideas and share my process with my clients. I am a visual person, so I think it's easier for others to understand how I work and how much time it takes to develop a great space when they can follow my process on social media.

Could you give some practical tips to someone who wants to become an interior designer?

You must keep learning because this is a world that is constantly evolving. Everyone can become an interior designer nowadays, so the more you know, the better equipped you are to create versatile and intelligent state-of-the-art spaces. Everybody does things differently, and that's great because it creates different styles.

Always make sure you double check everything you do. Any mistake you make is not only dangerous, but it can also be really expensive for you and your client. Most of all, you always have to believe in yourself for others to be able to believe in you.

17

○ www.OLinteriors.com
○ instagram.com/orenlasry

Start with a (business) plan

You might not have a business degree, and that's okay. Most people who work for themselves don't have one either. What you should have is at least a rough plan of how you'll make money in the future.

Every business is different, but the outline for each one is more or less the same: you must invest time and money to deliver a service or product to a customer, and you must have an idea of what channels are useful and effective to successfully accomplish your mission.

A business plan is an assumption of how you will operate in the future. Nothing that's written in a business plan is ever set in stone. Everything you outline is a desired state of how you'd like your company to function. A business plan is there to help you recognize certain factors you might have not thought about yet.

You don't need to worry about trying to make everything right because what makes for a successful business in the end is your ability to iterate your product until you find the right market-fit. Don't get caught up in details and most of all, don't allow your inner perfectionist discourage you. Let your inner visionary have a word instead.

You might be a one-woman business only in need of a laptop with internet access and your only investment might be your time. Then again, there's a possibility you'll need to have plenty of seed money to start, to get your business off the ground, so maybe you already have a savings account you can dip into or you have an investment from someone else. Your business plan should help you get an overview of what's to come. It should help you understand what your initial investments are, what tools you'll need, what services you'll offer, how you'll reach your customers, how they'll pay you, how much you should charge them, and all the other questions you'll need answered. Writing down any and all information available and filling in the gaps will help you determine when your business will break even and when you'll start making a profit.

19

One of my favorite resources to learn about writing a business plan is the **Business Model Generation,** a practical handbook that will help you understand the aspects of a business plan. Their business model canvas, which you can check out here (www.businessmodelgeneration.com/canvas/bmc), is the perfect tool for anyone who likes to sketch or use post-its to better visualize their endeavour.

Even if your plan is just for your own use, it will help you set your expectations for your future business. I believe that after you've filled in all the fields on your canvas, you'll better comprehend what steps to take next or who you need to contact to help you out.

The best news is yet to come: your business plan can also **make** you money. On one hand, you can apply to get a loan. Banks and investors will ask to see your business plan, so if you need a loan, that's where you'll have to start anyway. But the real good news is that your business plan can also lead to money, which you won't have to pay back.

You can read more about funding a little later, but now it's time for Maxie's story who wrote a business plan during her masters program and started her business before she even graduated. ◆

Maxie Matthiessen

SOCIAL ENTREPRENEUR, BERLIN

"You don't have to be a born entrepreneur. You can learn how to be an entrepreneur." Hearing these two sentences changed Maxie's life. She founded Ruby Cup, a social business to keep African girls in school, and established a buy-one-give-one model to reach her vision.

She speaks about what it takes to build an innovative business with a social purpose and what steps she took to build hers that, ultimately, changed lives.

What did you study and why?

I studied languages and culture. I've always been passionate about traveling and foreign cultures, but at the same time, I could never decide what exactly I wanted to do. I was also interested in business. For my masters, I chose to study international business and politics with a minor in social entrepreneurship; a program that focused on businesses with a social purpose.

The program has shaped how I view the world today. The first thing they taught us was that you don't have to be a born entrepreneur because no one is. Thinking and acting like an entrepreneur can be taught and learned just like anything else.

During my masters, I also learned that businesses don't have to be evil, but can serve their community for the better. Before the program, I didn't think any of this was possible, so it really opened my mind and made me consider, and eventually become, an entrepreneur.

What happened between your university diploma and your current career?

I was really inspired by the program and already started working on Ruby Cup during my studies. Part of the course was to write a business plan. There was an in-class competition and we won with our business plan; that gave me confidence and leverage that my idea had the potential to be turned into a viable business. Then, I approached the most capable women I knew and asked them if they were interested and wanted to join the team. Luckily, they agreed.

When we heard that the foreign ministry of Denmark was looking for interesting business ideas, we applied with the same business plan: we won that competition too. Although they didn't give us any money, they provided us with advice and connected us to the right people.

How did you come across the idea for your business?
People always think that innovative ideas must be new and unseen, but often it's just about changing the context of an already existing product that makes for innovative business models. For example, I was aware of the challenges many girls faced menstruating. When I was little, our neighbors collected money to buy tampons and pads for the girls in the refugee camps. Later, the UN published a report where they identified menstruation as a serious problem in third world countries because girls would often drop out of school to avoid the embarrassment of leaking. The way it was depicted made me wonder why no one has provided these girls with menstrual cups.

Follow your mission, money will always follow. Do what you have to do.

I've been using a menstrual cup for a long time myself. They are really popular in Denmark. So I didn't come up with a revolutionary discovery: I combined a problem with a solution I knew already existed and found a way to bridge the two. Like Steve Jobs always used to say, you have to connect the dots. That's basically what I did with Ruby Cup.

You changed your initial business model; how did that happen?
Initially, our business was headquartered in Nairobi. We founded the company based on the Tupperware-model: women sold to other women in Africa and were earning money while solving a problem. Truth is that we've constantly faced a financial problem because no matter how much we lowered the price of our product, girls in Kenya strictly couldn't afford to pay for it. We couldn't make it work.

We decided to move our company back to Europe and target women in the western markets instead. We changed our retail strategy to buy-one-give-one to keep true to our initial goal: to keep African girls in school. While our mission remained, our approach to solving the problem evolved.

What I believe is key to becoming a successful entrepreneur is to be able to test concepts and to not be afraid to try several different paths when your initial strategy doesn't work as expected. As for us, instead of having saleswomen sell Ruby Cups in Kenya, we now have an online shop and sell Ruby Cups in several stores that we've built a relationship with all across Europe.

23

What were your first steps to get Ruby Cup off the ground?
First, we had to develop the product. We approached a supplier of medical products who then connected us to suppliers we began to work with. The product went through several rounds of testing and multiple iterations. We then registered our company.

Our funding allowed us to go to Kenya and start our business without having to worry about our income for the whole of six months.

Every entrepreneur needs money in the beginning. We got funding because of all the competitions we won. I would advise anyone who has an idea to look for competitions and grants and apply. Not only does it help you to validate your business idea, but you will also receive valuable feedback that will eventually help you build a better company. We've received about 35K in total, which was enough for us to prove that we were able to establish a company. That's when investors started to get interested in our mission and our product.

One extremely valuable piece of advice I heard was upon our arrival in Kenya: we talked to the taxi driver and he assured us that when you follow your mission, money will always follow. Do what you have to do.

In the beginning, we had to find solutions to work around the fact that we didn't have much money in our bank account. I guess the taxi driver in Kenya was right given that after just a couple of months, we were approached by an investor.

How does it work for a white woman to establish a business in Africa?
Funny you ask, but it was much easier than you probably think. We tried to solve an actual problem that impacted peoples' lives: every man has a daughter and there wasn't an affordable solution that would help keep their girls in school.

On our first day in Nairobi, the taxi driver asked us why we were there. We were a little insecure to talk about such a secretive female issue with a man, so we said we had a product for female hygiene, which lasted ten years and helped girls during their menstruation. You cannot imagine how excited this man became. His reaction really surprised us. He immediately invited us to come to his village and give a Ruby Cup to every girl in the community.

Something similar happened when we applied for a visa. Usually, you wait for months and probably have to bribe someone, but when we told our story to the responsible officer, he was very supportive and we had our visas after just a couple of weeks. I think because we followed our mission and were able to convince a wide range of people about our cause, it wasn't as hard as we expected to start a business in Africa. We received numerous support along the way.

Can you talk a bit more about finding investors?
One day, a guy from London called me after he read something about us in the newspaper: 'I love your company! I want to invest! You should patent your product.' We had to slow him down and tell him that our product wasn't new, but had existed for decades and that the patents ran out a while ago, which is why we were able to start our company in the first place.

He was really enthusiastic and wanted to meet us. He came to Copenhagen and took us out to the most expensive restaurant. We went dancing and next thing you know, we were in business. He gave us 250K, which enabled us to really do more of what we wished for before there was any money. Of course as an investor, he wants to make money too, but he loves the social mission of Ruby Cup. We're not just business partners; we're friends.

What's your long-term vision for Ruby Cup and what do/will you do to reach your goals?

We want to become the preferred menstrual cup brand in the world, so there is a lot of work ahead of us. Menstrual cups are great, but they aren't a mainstream product yet and it's also something not many girls talk about.

Usually, our customers find us because they get frustrated with tampons and pads. We have a social mission, but we can only reach our aim if we manage to increase our numbers. We have an online store and are currently working on improving our SEO and doing some design changes. We try out a lot; for example, we've installed different landing pages to see which one works best. Then we try to connect with people who could write about us to increase the amount of links to our website. What we're especially excited about is that we're currently rolling out colorful Ruby Cups.

How do you represent yourself online? What platforms do you consider important?

We use Facebook, Twitter, and Instagram, and we are focusing on making better products and building relationships with ambassadors who can recommend us.

When I speak about myself, I always try to encourage people and share my insights that you can build a business that's financially viable while contributing to society.

Could you give some practical tips to someone who wants to become a social entrepreneur?

Don't over-think; start actively working on your idea. I have met so many people who are thinking, and thinking, and thinking, but what makes an exceptional entrepreneur isn't having an exceptional idea. It's about having an idea, realizing it, and iterating the concept until you find a way that sticks. Building a product means you have to test, iterate, and do it again and again. Many times.

So, first, register your company, then try to get funding, develop a great product, and register it. Then, start networking and doing PR.

Go to conferences and pitch your idea to anyone who will listen to you.

Take time to identify the right journalists who are interested in your field, then call them! Don't waste your time writing emails. Get in touch with people directly. PR is a lot of work and you have to take a lot of time to do it properly. ●

○ www.ruby-cup.com/en
○ twitter.com/maxie_maxie

Build
a financial buffer

Not everyone commits to creating their business full-time from day one, but there are several ways in which you can start. First off, you don't have to quit your job to write a business plan. Generally speaking, having a plan for what you want to do will help you understand how long it will take until you can live off your business.

There is no right or wrong way to start your own company; some people decide to work for themselves on side and keep their day-jobs. Others prefer to work hard and save up, then quit their jobs to strictly focus all of their energy on their own company. Often, these people set themselves a deadline for when they must earn enough money with their own business. It's mainly so they can focus on their long-term goals after they have left their secured job, while being able to support themselves in the meantime.

Your savings might cover your initial investments and also your living costs for a while, or you might find an investor to finance your investment costs, but that doesn't pay you a salary. When I interviewed all these wonderful women, I frequently asked about their financial situations and how long it took them to break even. For some, their businesses were up and running after only six months; others had been building theirs on side for years and only just recently started making money three or four years later.

Building a company takes time, and behind every "overnight success" is a story of entrepreneurs toiling away for years. It's essential to have enough money to be able to fully focus on building the business you envision, as well as being willing to take on projects that don't pay much, but are just the right credential to build your portfolio. Everyone has to start somewhere, so it's okay if the projects you take on in the beginning don't pay your bills straightaway. If you'd like to transition into a different role and do it as a self-employed entrepreneur, the best way to get there is to start taking on small projects on side and not only build up your savings account, but also your portfolio.

No one can tell you how long it will take to build your business and no one can give you a number to work towards. It all depends on how much you need to find peace of mind when your business doesn't make money from day one, or when you can't find clients for two or three months. You should have enough money in your bank account as a "security blanket" to be able to expand your business; it should enable you to work towards your long-term goals without having to worry where the money will come from that will pay your rent and food next week. ◆

Frances M Thompson

AUTHOR & COPYWRITER, AMSTERDAM

Craving a change from the corporate ladder in London and inspired by her location-independent partner, Frankie quit her job, sold most of her possessions, and hit the road to travel the world. She wanted to see what else the world had to offer and what other city she could eventually call her home.

Frankie now lives in the Netherlands where she works as a freelance copywriter, while eagerly working on her long-term goal; living off writing fiction. Here, she speaks more about savings and starting off as a freelancer without previous work experience in the field.

31

What did you study and why?

I studied what was called combined languages and learned French, German and Italian. I was good at languages and thought I should study something I was already good at. The fact that part of the program was a year abroad helped influence my decision too, as I've always loved travel.

It didn't take long for me to figure out that I wasn't necessarily interested in the careers that were common after the program; teaching or translating. I then decided to enroll in a masters program and study European law, which I happened to really enjoy, but I didn't want to become a lawyer. The part of my studies I enjoyed the most was writing and research.

It took a really long time until I finally admitted to myself and others that what I really wanted was to become a writer and a storyteller.

What happened between your graduation and your current career?

I became a corporate investigator, which I did for about seven years. I worked for consultancy firms and also within large multinational organizations, both of which allowed me to travel around Europe, the Middle East and North America. It was a very interesting job and I really enjoyed the type of work I did, but at the same time, I wasn't able to travel for pleasure as much as I wanted.

In 2009, I started blogging about my local area in London, Shepherd's Bush. I was looking for a creative outlet and within a few years, I started to wonder if I could actually make writing my main source of income. Around the same time, I became active on social media. I started meeting people with similar interests. It was all very exciting as I realized the potential of the Internet to open up opportunities to me.

What made you decide to quit your job and start writing full-time?
I met my partner in 2010. Originally from Sydney, Australia, he had been location-independent for more than ten years. He was a great source of inspiration and definitely had an influence on my final decision because at the time, I was very anxious about freelancing. I didn't want to just take a few months off and go backpacking; I wanted to make an actual lifestyle change.

32

I always try to over-deliver. My goal is for my clients to remember me, for good reasons! I try to keep in touch and to stay informed with what they're doing. It's always nice to congratulate them on their own special successes.

About a year before we hit the road, I started taking on small copywriting jobs on the side to build my portfolio. I looked for jobs on websites like Elance and PeoplePer-Hour and I wrote copy for my boyfriend's company and the companies of my friends. I was really just testing the waters to see what was possible. I gradually saw that it was feasible to make money that way, and when I had enough savings on side, I quit my job.

What were your first steps to make a career as a freelance copywriter possible?
I saved up about six months worth of salary just to make sure I could survive for a while. Also, we traveled to cheaper places like Morocco and Thailand, and that helped make my money go further.

In the beginning, I also did guest articles and posts for free. I was focusing on gaining references and trying out different styles. Probably the only thing I didn't try was cold-calling. It's not ideal for an author, but I've never liked rejection, and that would have made me insecure and lower my self-confidence in the long run.

It took me about a year to find four or five regular clients, of which about half came through job boards such as Elance. At the time, it felt like everything was moving very slowly, but now I know that building a viable freelance career after only a year was much faster than how long it took other people I talked to. Before we left for our travels, I started a second blog and dedicated it entirely to traveling. I published new posts almost every day and I was lucky that this grew very quickly. This also gave me some new opportunities to travel and to boost my profile and portfolio online. I quickly realized one of the key benefits of freelancing was how flexible I could be with my time. I used what free time I had to make a first attempt and write a book.

Before, while living in London, although writing a book had always been my dream, I always thought that I didn't have enough time. I now know this to be rubbish! Of course I had time, but I filled it with other things: seeing friends, going out all night, going on city breaks and holidays. Freelancing made me reassess how I spent my time and traveling gave me the confidence to actually commit and focus on what was really important to me.

How much money were you making in the beginning?
In the first month, I probably only earned a couple hundred dollars. In the second month, I think I doubled that and by the end of the first year, I was earning between $1,000 – $2,000 per month (before tax). It was still a fraction of my old salary in London, but it was enough to have a good life in Southeast Asia.

After about 18 months, I was comfortable with the income I was earning each month. Now, years later, I'm still not earning as much as I used to in my previous job, but I'm still saving and I'm *happy*. Money isn't a focus of mine at the moment; I'm happy to spend less in order to make my money go further. What's more important for

33

me is having enough time to do the things I love and to build my business as an author, i.e. to write more books!

How do you find clients and how do they find you?
Generally speaking, I have three sources of income: my blog, my books, and my copywriting. Copywriting work comes mostly through word-of-mouth, but I also get copywriting jobs through my website, sometimes through LinkedIn, and occasionally through Twitter or Facebook.

Then I have clients who come to me through my blog. In the last year, I've seen a definite increase in my earnings through blog collaborations, which after five years of blogging just for the love of it is great. This is something I hope to continue to nurture in 2015 as I collaborate with other bloggers on a few campaigns. One, in particular, is a project called *Must Love Festivals* whereby a group of bloggers go 'festival-hopping' around the world and portray to people that festivals aren't just about mud and music, but they're about people, traditions, art, culture, food and most importantly, brilliant stories! It's important we bloggers show how professional we are and how we have unique storytelling skills which brands can harness. However, copywriting is still my 'bread and butter' as the work is more reliable and regular.

How do you make your clients happy? How do you make sure they hire you again?
I always try to over-deliver. My goal is for them to remember me, for good reasons! In terms of getting hired again, I try to keep in touch, without bombarding them, and to stay informed with what they're doing. It's always nice to congratulate them on their own special successes.

You have to be realistic though. Not everybody wants to hire you forever and of course, it's always possible that you will lose a client or two along the way. For that reason, I've learned that it helps to always be proactive with a new or potential client. When people ask you to do one thing, you can always look at their business in general, try to identify how you could add value to their business, and suggest some additional services.

I'm now much more relaxed about being a freelancer than I was years ago. I know that I can always go back to PeoplePerHour, if I have to, although I haven't used a job board for nearly two years. I'm used to preparing for periods of both 'feast' and 'famine,' and whenever I do have a quiet period, I don't panic. In fact, I rejoice as it means I can dedicate more time to work on my books.

How long did it take you to make your books and your blog a viable source of income?

At the moment, my books only make up a very small percentage of my income. I guess it's about five to ten percent. I'm an independent author and publish the books myself, and therefore, I treat each book as a 'business asset' and each one has overheads.

I'm still in debt with my last book because I haven't yet made back what I paid for the editing, proofreading, and the cover design. Currently, each book costs me around € 500 in costs, but once those costs are made back, the profit is all mine and I can make profit from my books for the rest of my life. That's not a bad business model in the long run! Also, the more books I write and publish, the more I sell.

I consider living off my books as a long-term goal. As for now, I pay my bills from freelance copywriting, though the money I get through my blog is nice to have too! I would love to monetize my blog more, but it's never been a focus for me. It was my first creative outlet and it remains a labor of love. I try to blog three or four times a week and I still find it very valuable for not only building my online profile, but exercising my creative muscles. It's not something I've initially done to make money.

How do you market your books?

I find readers through Amazon, where my books retail, and on my blog. Social media is useful for marketing, but gets me very few direct sales. In fact, I don't like to use it to try and sell books, apart from when I'm running a promotion, which I like to do regularly because it helps boost sales and awareness of my books. That said, social media is a great way to build an audience and speak to your readers directly. I'm also very active on Goodreads.com, both as an author and as a reader. That's one of the ways I try to be in a place where active readers are naturally, rather than trying to sell to people who don't read books, which doesn't make any sense to me!

I'm also working on building my newsletter list. I'm very lucky that I have a good engagement and response rate from my newsletter readers, and I think that's because I'm not just selling to them; I'm talking with them, helping them, or sharing something useful.

— 36

Saying, 'Buy my book,' is not appealing to anyone; you have to share something interesting and this will help them see you as a person they want to hear from again. Then, maybe further down the line, they will remember, 'Oh, she had some interesting ideas, maybe I should try one of her books.'

At the time, it felt like everything was moving very slowly, but now I know that building a viable freelance career after only a year was much faster than how long it took other people I talked to.

For example, in November I published *30 Days of NaNoWriMo Inspiration* to try and encourage those who have always wanted to write a book. It's a cause close to my heart and it was wonderful to receive emails at the end of the month from people who had given it a go or who had won. They would say to me, 'Thanks so much, I signed up to your newsletter to stay in touch, or I downloaded your book to see what happened to your first NaNoWriMo project.' Of course, I've also tried many marketing tactics that didn't work. I tried a book tour that was hosted on several blogs, but it was a waste of money because half of the blogs were not reader blogs.

I also use Amazon to market my books in a number of ways. You have to be savvy about your keywords so you're found easily by those who are searching for a book like yours, you have to make sure your blurb is great, and you have to have some good, genuine reviews. I use a great team of beta-readers to get early reviews, and I also offer free review copies to anyone who promises to review one of my books on Amazon or Goodreads. There are also a few ways you can use Amazon to promote your book by running price reduction promotions or even by giving one of your books away for free for a limited period of time. There are a few rules and regulations surrounding this (you have to sell exclusively on Amazon), but when you're just getting started, this is definitely something I would recommend experimenting with.

Having said all this, I believe that at the moment, the number one thing that will help me sell more books is writing and publishing more books. I don't think much is going to happen until I have written at least five. I'm currently writing and publishing on average one book every year, but I'm also working on beating this goal!

Can you give some practical tips to someone who wants to become a freelance copywriter?

If your aim is to make money with writing, then you have to be very flexible. You have to understand the different styles of writing people require and you have to be able to take criticism well and be able to self-edit your work to its best possible standard. Make producing quality work your number one goal. And don't forget to have your own platform, be it a blog, a column on Medium or maybe a book, and publish as many examples of your best work as you can and share it proudly. Future clients will want to see examples of your work, so make sure you have a good, varied selection.

I also think you need to consider thorough research. A huge part of my job is researching a new-to-me topic or fact-checking something for an article I'm ghostwriting. Get accustomed to research and you'll deliver better work for it.

You also have to be flexible in how you find work and gain regular clients. I first started looking for work on various job boards while also building a portfolio by publishing guest posts on other blogs for free. Although I know that many people are against working for free and using platforms like the ones I did, I can't dissuade anyone from using them because it has worked for me.

If your bigger aim is to write books, then start writing NOW: nothing will make you a better writer than writing regularly. And don't underestimate the value of writing for yourself. I've just started keeping a private journal again after a ten year absence and it's liberating and therapeutic to write for my eyes only.

One of the hardest things I learned as a freelancer and an independent author was how to promote myself, but your true fans and the clients who are potentially interested want to hear about your accomplishments, so don't be afraid to share them gracefully with your network: be it on Facebook, LinkedIn, or Twitter.

My last piece of advice is to be patient and to persevere. People now contact me through my website, but that took years to build up, and while my copywriting business is flourishing, I'm still at the outset of my journey as an author. I'm reminding myself that I had to start at the beginning as a freelancer and I'm doing the same thing now as an indie author. We all have to start at the beginning, but who knows where we'll end up if we just stick with it! ●

O www.fmthompson.com
O twitter.com/bushbirdie

Make yourself a website

Whenever you meet someone and they find you interesting, they'll most likely google you afterwards. Before they search you, remember that you are the only person who can influence what they'll find.

What they should find is a website that tells them about your background, shows your references, and explains what they can hire you for. Even if you run a business and have a product page, you should still have a personal website, or at least have an "about me" page.

Your website is your virtual business card, so it's in your hands how you want to present yourself to potential clients. This is your chance to establish what you want to be known for and what projects you want to be working on in the future.

Before you start panicking that you don't know anything about web-design, let alone how to program a website, you should stop yourself right there because you're already thinking ahead. Take a piece of paper and a pen and write down how you'll want to structure the content.

The most basic website should have an "about me," a section where you describe your references, list the services you provide or products you offer, and explain how people can work with you. Don't forget to include a contact form or make your email address and your phone number clearly visible so potential clients can easily contact you.

When you write copy for your own website, you should think about how people will read and interpret it. Let me explain: everything you publish on your website is a potential Google query. No one will type in Google "designer who knows how to use Photoshop," but it's very likely that your potential client will google "designer who can retouch pictures." When you write copy for your website, try to focus on your strengths and not what tools or programs you use; it's very unlikely your client knows about these things. They just know what they want, so write the way you want people to find you on Google. Complicated terminology won't benefit you.

41

When you showcase your references, try to do it in a way that's relatable. Don't just say who the client was you worked with, but also explain the successes you accomplished and what you did to help your client reach those goals. It's a missed opportunity if you only state the client's name because the one thing that distinguishes you from everyone else is the way you approach projects. They want to know your strategies and your process, so be open; your future clients will appreciate it.

If you want to be heard, increase your sales or establish yourself within an audience. **Don't tell your readers who you are, but tell them what you can do for them.** Show them what problems you can help them solve. There's a high possibility they'll listen to you and hear your voice much louder.

Once you've finalized the copy for your website and had someone else proofread it (!), it's time to think about the technical aspects of building a website.

Personally, I'm a fan of systems I fully control myself where I don't need to call someone to help me decipher and navigate the site, which is why I've recently switched to Squarespace. Their customer support is amazing and you don't need to be technical in any way to make the website you want. A big plus is that they give you your domain name for free once you've subscribed to their services for a year.

Other services you might feel comfortable using are Wordpress, Wix, or Weebly.

All these services offer templates, which you can adjust to your needs. When picking a theme, think about the content you've previously mapped out and what aspects are most important for people to see. If you are a musician, make sure people will hear your music before they do anything else on your website. If you have your own online shop, look for a template that gives you the opportunity to feature your favorite products or any holiday promotions first and then allow people click further. Or, if you are an online consultant, make it easy for people to understand what you specialize in. Think about what you want people to see first and build everything else around it. And also, don't forget to check how your website looks on mobile devices.

The one investment I would advise you to make is hiring a professional photographer or asking someone you know to help you. Your website must be visually appealing; otherwise, no one will read your well-crafted copy and that would be a shame. Think of a concept and try to make every image you use look good next to the other. Your website needs to showcase your special talents, so unless you're a travel blogger, don't use images of you on holiday. Think about how you want others to perceive you, which should be honest yet professional, and ask someone to take pictures of you to show you in that light. ◆

43

Diana Ovezea

TYPE DESIGNER, AMSTERDAM

Being a type designer is not about quick wins and it's definitely not about quick successes: it's a long process with long-term goals and uncountable failures. In 2013, Diana published her first font family "Paiper," her first big success after graduating at the Royal Academy of Arts in The Hague, which is available in Gestalten's type foundry. In her interview, Diana discusses patience, gaining self-confidence, credibility and availability.

What did you study and why?

After I finished high school, I wanted to either become a lawyer or a psychologist. I then found out about graphic design and it felt like a combination of the two. As a lawyer, you have to be able to diplomatically reason your decisions. As a psychologist, you have to listen to people and analyze them to be able to figure out the right solutions that complements their personality. While graphic design is a creative profession, you have to have strong interpersonal skills and pitch your product just like lawyers do in their day-to-day. It felt like the right choice.

Then I discovered my fascination for type design because when you create fonts, you create systems. It's not just about designing nice looking letters because letters make words, words make sentences and sentences make pages; it all has to look good and function in the micro but also in the macro level.

What happened between your university diploma and your current career?

I already started working in my third year of undergrad. One of my teachers hired me to work in their small design agency.

That really boosted my self-confidence. I was able to apply what I've learned about what it meant to be a professional designer. What you learn in school is often very different from the experiences you gain in the real world when people pay you for your services. The real challenge is not to lose your spirit and spark when things aren't as smooth as you expect them to be. I stayed with the agency for about two years and took the time to choose and prepare for a masters program.

After finishing my masters at the Royal Academy of Arts in The Hague, I wanted to stay in the city. There weren't many jobs, so I decided to immediately become self-employed.

What were the reasons you took the leap and started freelancing?
When you take the chance to do a postgrad, you learn so much about how much you don't know. It breaks you because you feel like you don't know anything and that you're far from being able to call yourself a professional. I wanted to stay in the Netherlands because there are so many resources, organizations, museums, and events to learn from.

As a foreigner who doesn't speak the language, it turned out to be very difficult to find a job. I needed to make a living as fast as possible. A former employer from Austria offered me some work if I could do it as a freelancer, so I jumped at the chance and started working as a freelance graphic designer.

I guess the lack of job opportunities made me consider becoming self-employed and hunger made me actually do it.

What were your first steps to make it happen?
I had so many questions! I talked to anyone and everyone I could get ahold of; people I admired for what they were doing. I talked to people who had their own studios and did projects I liked and who have been in business for 10 or even 20 years. Talking to them and listening to their stories helped me gain the confidence that I could also be a freelancer and maybe even become successful if I dedicate all of my energy to making this work.

But even talking to people didn't necessarily help me feel 'real.' I needed something to give me the feeling I'm a professional and not just a student surfing on the freelance wave. I bought myself some tools and organized a big table. Then I started looking for an actual office space so that I could have the feeling that I was 'going to work.'

I think my main problem was that I didn't feel like I existed on the map of typography, so to take the next step, I made myself a website where I displayed my references and a portfolio. I needed the feeling that I had something tangible that would allow me to approach people.

I reached out to the staff at the Royal Academy to let them know that I was still in the city. People always assume that when you move to a country to study, you'll return to your home country once you graduate. I decided to stay, so I also started learning Dutch.

I think my biggest mistake was to think that setting up my own business would only take about six months. At one point, I was even considering to look for different types of jobs, such as babysitting, but I figured that instead of wasting my time strategizing about how to 'survive' this month, I should focus on the long term goal. This meant that I had to take advantage of my savings. Nevertheless, I decided to do it anyway and considered it as an investment in my own future.

What was your first project?

Just as I was questioning my abilities and decisions the most, I got my first big client. Gestalten approached me to create a font for their type foundry. They found my work on Behance and liked my style.

Type foundries work the same way as publishing houses and music publishers; they don't necessarily pay you immediately, but you earn royalties based on the actual sales that they give you twice a year. Although it's not immediate income, and definitely not a

> Make a big effort to celebrate every little success and every little achievement.

quick win, it's a way to build a passive income. You need several typefaces, just as you need several books, to build a portfolio so you're eventually able to live off your work.

Most type designers work on client work on a daily basis, and they design fonts on the side to accumulate a passive income.

Although creating 'Paiper' didn't pay anything to start with, it kept me busy and gave me a purpose. It was a very conscious investment of my time because I felt that I was pouring my time into building a future. Releasing a typeface has given me credibility and basically put me on the map, at least in my own perception.

I believe there is a difference between designers who work on type designs and designers who have actually managed to release a typeface. They had the guts to put their work out there for the world to see, scrutinize, critique, and hopefully, admire. In the end, that's what makes you a professional; unless you generate income with the work you produce, it's just another hobby.

48

How long does it take to release a typeface?

I worked on 'Paiper' for about six months, but it can take two, three, or even six years. If designing a typeface is your only commitment, you can work faster. The time period is dependent on the scope of the project: how many languages it should cover, what technical features it should include, and other components that go into development. Most of the time, designing typefaces is something a type designer can't afford to do full-time.

You have to test fonts a lot: design, print, test, ask for feedback, iterate, and then repeat these steps multiple times before you create a typeface that's ready to be released. You have to create many different examples of where and how your new font can be applied to prove the font really works, as well as to inspire the potential buyer to purchase it. It takes a while and then at the end, you have to deal with the technical requirements. You can either self-publish a font, just as self-published writers or musicians would, or you can try to find a foundry to release the type for you.

Life is not school: you can't learn 'in advance,' you can only learn in retrospect.

How do you make money?

Doing your own thing is great, but if there is no money coming in, you quickly lose your energy because you keep worrying about your income and thus, your basic needs.

Last summer, I was able to stop working as a graphic designer. Now I only work on type-related projects. I teach once a week at the university where I graduated. Once a week, I work in one of my former teacher's type foundry and I run a course where I teach calligraphy to beginners who are passionate about learning a new skill.

To sum things up, I have a couple of income streams, which keeps my day-to-day diverse and exciting.

How do you find clients and how do they find you?

I believe that you have to go to conferences and events and actually talk to people. Let them know that you're available for projects. Just don't try too hard; this comes off negatively.

You simply can't lock yourself in and hope that someone will approach you. People will assume that you're busy, so you really have to let them know that you're actually looking for work. You must also feel confident about the work you produce and be willing to talk about it.

How do you represent yourself online? What platforms do you consider important?

I have my own website and I use Behance as a portfolio because that's where people often look for designers. Nevertheless, having your own website is essential because it shows that you're serious about what you do. I also think that it's important for other people to write about you. That's, obviously, something you can't influence; all you can do is make your work as public and as visible as possible.

I'm also involved with typedrawers.com and www.typophile.com where I regularly contribute to various discussions. I think it's important to give back to the community and help out wherever you can.

I'm also a very active meetup.com member. I'm involved with two groups: one is to meet like-minded others and discuss typography once in a while and the other meetup is one I organize myself.

My friend and I started a calligraphy course together, so we even make money with our meetup group.

Could you give some practical tips to someone who wants to become a type designer?

Make a big effort to celebrate every little success and every little achievement. Always look at where you were last month and where you are now. Don't compare yourself too much to others. Instead, as Rob Symington said, only compare yourself to the previous versions of yourself.

In a world that is so focused on instant gratification, type design is on the other end of the spectrum. You really must love type design because otherwise, you'll suffer. There are so many obstacles, so you have to get used to failing and failing regularly.

I wish somebody would have told me how long it takes to build a business. I expected to be on my feet and running within a few months, but you have to plan that it will take about a year, if not longer.

Take the time and invest in your future. Do projects that will make you happy in the long run, even if it sometimes means that you say 'no' to a project. Most of all, find a purpose for yourself. If you are an over-thinker, an overachiever, or a perfectionist, then stop thinking and start *doing*. Life is not school: you can't learn 'in advance,' you can only learn in retrospect. You must start doing things to learn to understand.

Last but not least, don't be shy and let people know you're available for projects. People don't know that unless you tell them. ●

○ www.ovezea.com
○ twitter.com/typemuseum

51 —

Share your work

You know how it seems almost impossible to get a job when you get out of university because everyone says you must have work experience to get work experience? Now, with projects, it's sort of the same. You need to have references within the style of projects you want to be involved with in order to have more projects within that same style for the future. At least, that is, unless you're just damn lucky!

If you were stuck in the last chapter thinking you didn't have any projects you could show, it's time you become your own client. Just because you call yourself a professional graphic designer, a copywriter, or a photographer doesn't mean you always work on projects you want to be working on. Just because you see other people's work and admire them for what they do, doesn't mean that those are the projects that pay their rent.

If you ever wondered where the phrase "fake it till you make it" came from, this is probably it. As I said in the beginning, you need to build the business you want to work for yourself, which also means you need to build a portfolio that will help you get the projects, and ultimately build the business, you want! The more people get to see your work – the type you want to be associated with – the more beneficial it will be for you.

Once you decide to share your work, it's time to choose the right platform. We often use social media in a different context because we show what we like, but we rarely share what we're working on. We post pictures of our family and friends, we take pictures while we're on vacation, and because everyone loves food, we occasionally share a picture of what's on our plate. It might feel unnatural to stop yourself while working and take a picture of what you do and upload it to Instagram, write a short article for your blog while you're on it, or share a quick thought that crossed your mind on Twitter. Documenting the work process takes practice and some getting used to, but it's the best tool to show and spread what you do. The medium that's right for you is one where you feel comfortable and preferably one you own, such as your personal blog or a newsletter. I personally believe that no one needs to be on every platform and try to be present everywhere. One or two social media channels, if done properly, are more than enough. You can still share pictures of your loved ones on Facebook, just mention your work there from time to time too. You can read more about social media platforms in the chapter, "Go social."

53

If you're not a social media native because you don't like showing pictures of your private life, then that's even better because it might be easier for you to look at social media from a professional point of view. You won't have to switch focus of how you use social media; you can start from scratch and share your work without distracting your followers with pictures of people they don't know.

Generally speaking, using social media for professional purposes starts with finding the right outlet. Choosing your medium is important because if you try to force it and use one where you constantly have to step out of your comfort zone, you might not keep up sharing your work for long. If you're not any good at writing short captions, then leave Twitter to the people who are. If you prefer writing long articles, share it on LinkedIn, @Medium, or your blog. If words aren't your forte, focus on visuals and share your work on Instagram, Tumblr, or Pinterest. And lastly, if you know you're a great speaker and texts or images don't do you justice, tape yourself and start a vlog on Youtube.

Now, consistency is the key. You can share your work once, but it probably won't have any lasting effect. If you do it regularly, such as once a week or every other week, it will become a habit and it's more likely you'll keep up sharing. I know I said you should try to stop yourself in the middle of working to document your progress and show it publicly, but you can also reflect on your process once a week and then share what has kept you busy for the past seven days. I've personally come to experience that a deadline, regularity, and social pressure helps a lot to keep you on the ball.

What suits you best might be different from what best suits me or your friend. When I first published my website, I decided to send out a newsletter once a week. But not just once a week: I set myself a deadline to send out a newsletter every Monday. Having this deadline and having it on a particular day has been a helpful tactic to keep me going. So, you have to figure out what works best for you and go from there.

Let's go back to being your own client; as Oren already said, you must work "on" your business and not just "in" your business. Working on your business means that you try to develop towards a direction you're interested in for you to eventually earn the money you deserve for all of your hard efforts. Building a company you want to work for takes time, and you can only get there if you invest time to build it. Whether you're able to invest two hours a day or half a day every week, dedicate time to participate in projects you're passionate about.

Be your own client, share the work you're proud of, do it regularly, and the rest will fall into place eventually. Check out Lauren's story to understand how she's finally getting the kind of work she always wanted. ◆

Lauren Randolph

PHOTOGRAPHER, LOS ANGELES

You might know @laurenlemon from Instagram: more than 240,000 people do since she's one of Instagram's suggested members. Lauren is a professional photographer who now gets her jobs not just because people who loved working with her referred her to others; she gets jobs that suit her style because someone found her images online and liked her persona. For a long time, she struggled with the business aspect of being a freelancer, which is why she signed up with a representative. Here, she tells a bit more about working "on" her business by being her own client .

What did you study and why?

First, I started studying journalism because I was interested in magazines and advertising, but after a year, I switched to fine arts with a major in photography. I was still interested in advertising and magazines: I just didn't want to come up with taglines and editorials.

What happened between university and your current career?

I already started working as a photographer while I was in school. I mostly photographed events and shot local musicians and restaurants.

After graduation, I moved to LA and because I thought I needed a secure part time job, I started looking for secretary positions. I never got a job as a secretary in the end, and I can only explain why because of what happened at one of the interviews: the HR manager took me aside and said that she'd love to hire me, but my CV with all my references from school read like a resumé of a photographer. She said she knew that if someone would offer me a photography job, I would leave. She was right. I only considered these jobs because I thought I could only survive if I had a regular income. Also, my sister nudged me that if I would spend half of the time I put into searching for secretarial jobs looking for photography jobs, I would get to do what I really want to be doing. So I dared the jump!

What were the first photography jobs you had?

In the beginning, I only did really small jobs. I said 'yes' to everything that came my way and paid: retouching old photographs, shooting headshots, small bands, weddings, and I took on a lot of assisting jobs that enabled me to work with other photographers.

In the first few months, I didn't have that many jobs and I definitely wasn't able to choose what I wanted to do. Luckily, I had a credit card, so I charged a lot on that and paid it back every time I got some work.

At some point, people started recommending me. So after the first few months, many of the jobs I had I got through word-of-mouth.

Don't let me mislead you; it's not as though I had much money coming in. My sister and I lived in a one-bedroom apartment and we tried to live as cheaply as possible. At least we were both doing what we were passionate about.

How long did it take you to be able to choose your clients?

Definitely more than four years. In 2014, I have finally been able to choose what clients I want to work with and I was able to turn down the smaller jobs when they weren't interesting to me and didn't pay much.

For a very long time, I only assisted other photographers and the work I presented on my website was work I shot for fun when I was out with friends. Now I'm finally getting jobs because people like my style: the carefree spirit. They like my personal approach to photography.

What's something you've been struggling with as a freelance photographer?

Last year, I realized what kind of jobs really suit me and that I can call myself a photographer without feeling like I'm half faking it. I just signed with a commercial representative to help me with the administrative side of my business.

I'm a confident photographer. I know I take good pictures, but I didn't go to business school and I lack confidence when negotiating rates and budgets. Many times, when I got an email from an amazing client I really wanted to work with, instead of jumping around excitedly, I would almost have a panic attack because I knew I had to put on a poker face and be businesswoman Lauren. It's not easy for me to state my day rate, how much I charge for my assistants, and then negotiate every time they tell me their budget is below my initial estimate.

All I want is to do good work and shoot awesome photos. Negotiating really makes me feel uncomfortable. I always consulted fellow photographers and asked them how much they would charge. Now I can call my representative because she's familiar with the budgets in the industry.

59

I know of a lot of photographers who move to LA and immediately start reaching out to representatives because some agencies only take you seriously when you are represented by someone else. To me, it felt more logical to market myself to get jobs and not market myself to get an agent; a representative wasn't going to give me money to pay my rent. They usually charge 20-30% of your creative charge, which is why

> I've always shared my work online and tried to show it to as many people as possible. It's a free marketing tool; you just have to use it.

I didn't waste my time looking for one. I always thought that one day, when the time is right, a representative would approach me, which is what eventually happened.

My current agent approached me while I was on tour in Europe. I really liked her and her assistant, who I'm on the phone with probably as often as I am with my representative. It was important to me to work with someone who can play hard, but at the same time is approachable, responsive, and easy to talk to. My agent represents about ten other photographers who all have their own niche. I know that she's been showing my work to different agencies.

Now when I get a job, I have someone to consult with who I trust.

Sometimes, my agent or her assistant do the creative calls together with me and the clients too. That's really helpful.

How do you find clients and how do they find you?
Mostly through social media. I've always shared my work online and tried to show it to as many people as possible. It's a free marketing tool; you just have to use it.

Before Instagram came along, I'd been posting to Flickr almost daily. I've sold some stock photos through Flickr too.

I can recommend the Getty Calculator, which I use every time someone asks me for an image from my archives: www.gettyimages.co.uk/pricecalculator/sb10069475ab-001

What did you do when you didn't have enough work to keep you busy?
When you are a freelancer, you don't know what's coming next. I've learned that having a savings account is essential. Even in times when I have a lot to do, I'm trying to save up and not spend all of my earnings. I now know that there might be times without many projects.

Instead of jumping around excitedly when I got an email from an amazing potential client, I would almost have a panic attack because I knew I had to put on a poker face and become businesswoman Lauren.

A couple of years ago, I had a moment where my credit card was used to the maximum and I had no idea when I would land my next job; that's when I got my first big commercial job, as if the universe knew. As soon as I got paid, I paid off all my debts. However, I can't say that was the big breakthrough because after this one job, I went back to assisting jobs.

When I started off, I tried to be social and go to as many interesting events as possible. I also went on photo walks with fellow photographers and we took pictures of one another.

Now, when I have time, I always try to come up with an idea for a personal project. I organize a stylist, the settings and everything else I need, and then I shoot a series of five to ten images I usually publish to my website and my social media channels to add to my portfolio.

Is there something you're scared of?

Honestly, I wouldn't want to do anything else but be a photographer. Nevertheless, being a freelancer is a constant state of fear because there are times without any jobs and there is always the possibility that I get injured. And then what?!

My plan is to make a proper savings strategy, put money away, and take care of my retirement plan. I want to set myself long-term goals and decide what I want to achieve in five or ten years. I usually plan one month ahead. It's all fun and games because I get to travel and I really enjoy myself. But then, I always have to remember that what I do is my career, my business, and that it's the business that has to take care of my needs down the road when I eventually can't work the way I do now.

How do you represent yourself online? What platforms do you consider important?

I use Facebook, Instagram, Tumblr, Twitter, and I'm always trying out new photo apps, if only to reserve my name, @laurenlemon. Social media is important to me.

I'm very personable online because it allows me to reach out to the kind of clients who are interested and want to work with me. They see and like the fact that I'm an adventurous, free-spirited person and not just someone to get the job done. For example, Instagram is more of a private diary of mine where I capture concerts I like, adventures I go on, and people I meet along the way.

I didn't want to be just 'Lauren Randolph Photography.' I know a lot of people who don't like blurring the lines between their professional and their personal lives. For me, the approach has worked! My online persona is my professional persona and that's how I get clients.

What are some tips you would give to someone who wants to start off as a freelance photographer?

Never stop shooting. Even if no one pays you for shooting, you must continue doing so every day. Now with smartphones and Instagram, it's much easier to keep taking pictures, so take advantage of it. If people see your photographs, they'll assume that's what you do and that you're doing well. Then, when they hear of a job that suits your style, they're far more likely to think of you and recommend you. ●

○ www.photolauren.com
○ instagram.com/laurenlemon

Lauren Randolph • Photographer, Los Angeles

Leave your inner perfectionist at the door

Okay, so you'd like to share your work, but it's never exactly the way you want it to be, right? You feel you're not good enough and everyone else's work is better than yours: sounds familiar? It's time you fire your inner perfectionist.

First, sharing your work doesn't necessarily mean that you're only sharing the final outcome and it also doesn't mean that everything you share must be perfect. As Austin Kleon said in his book *Show Your Work*, "Think process, not product." Sharing your progress might be easier for you to do because "progress" and "process" insinuate that your work is not yet complete and thus, not perfect. When something isn't done, no one expects it to be perfect either and people will support you along the way; if not, then fire that friend too.

If you're only just starting something new, you're most likely feeling insecure about sharing your progress. I believe that if you're open about your learning process, people are always very supportive of your new endeavor. The good news is that if you're only starting out, you most likely don't have many followers just yet. The people who like you will support you on your journey and your number of followers, if that's important to you, will rise too. Keep in mind that the world is big and that what you do won't reach everyone's ears. I've been sharing my work actively on all social media channels for years and I still have friends who have no idea what I'm actually doing. People are busy and no one judges you as closely as you do yourself. Always remember that.

It might be easier for you to start sharing once you make it an official project. For example, have you ever stumbled upon one of the "#365DaysProject" or "#30DaysofHappiness" projects on Instagram? There are so many ventures out there for people to document their process and acknowledge that they're not perfect, but they're learning and getting better every day. See them for yourself to get inspired.

65

You might not start your business tomorrow, as in terms of monetizing your passion, but you can lay out the foundation for your business. Start growing an audience first so when you eventually decide for it all to become a business, it will only be a matter of monetizing it and not a matter of finding your audience or first customers.

Personally, what has always helped me is getting other people involved in the work I do. I know myself very well, and I know that if I would be solely responsible for the outcome, I'd probably stand in my own way most of the time. What I do to overcome my inner perfectionist is I share the responsibility with someone I trust. For instance, I work with an editor who looks over the flow of my texts and catches any typos and mistakes. If I then later find mistakes, I don't feel discouraged because I know that it wasn't just on my shoulders to catch them. Two pair of eyes are always better; also, don't forget, it's the internet! You can delete old posts if you become the next Oprah and don't want to show where you came from. Leave your inner perfectionist at the door, start sharing today, and listen to what Akilah has to say. She said "goodbye" to her inner perfectionist a while ago, so take a look at where she is today. ◆

Akilah Hughes

COMEDIAN & VLOGGER, BROOKLYN

Big dreams, big visions and big ambitions – that's Akilah, obviously! You might have stumbled upon her Youtube channel where she talks about everything from her obsession with hair to interracial dating. What she really wants is to become the next "Oprah." She speaks about persistency and practice, and how important it is to overcome your inner critic.

What did you study and why?
I did an independent major in college in broadcasting and speech communications with a focus in mass communications – mostly because my life goal was to become Oprah.

You started your blog while you were at university. How did that happen?
Youtube launched while I was still in college, so I used it for projects. I had a friend who blogged and her site slowly transitioned from written content to mostly vlogs. I admired her and her channel and decided to do something similar.

In the beginning I copied her style, but wasn't necessarily good at it. Then I created a new style: my style. I was persistent and kept making videos. I aimed at making at least one every week. So far, I've made over 200 videos; some better than others.

When I was at university, no one thought you could ever become your own production company. Youtube back then was really new. I spent a lot of time googling things like, 'How do I do this in Adobe Premiere?' and just kept researching and teaching myself until I got better at it. Now, I produce YouTube videos with my friend, Tim, who shoots and cuts all my takes.

What happened between your university diploma and your current career?
Well, I didn't become Oprah.

Ever since I graduated in 2010, I've had a bunch of different jobs. I even moved to Florida to be a cast member at Disney World before taking on various marketing jobs back in my hometown. Then it was time for me to get serious about getting where I wanted to be and I moved to New York. I've worked a lot with social media and only recently, I've started moving into being a producer for television.

So, how did you make the transition and made your hobby your main source of income?
I started making Youtube videos in 2012. A majority of them were short, sketch comedy videos. I'd been doing it for almost two years before one of the videos, 'Meet your first black girlfriend,' a video about interracial dating, got picked up. I think the fact that so many people could relate to the content helped make it so popular. So far, the video's had more than a million views.

68

I slowly started making Youtube a bigger part of my career. Being persistent has paid off and helped in building an audience. After about a year, I had 8,000 subscribers, which is not huge by any means, but it's enough to make a video go viral if enough of those people share it.

Now, with the internet, people are okay when things aren't perfect. At least as long as they're constantly getting better.

Having made the sort of content I post on Youtube, I get a lot of requests for interesting projects. Eventually, one day someone said, 'Come and make videos for us.' That's how it all started. But don't forget, that took two years!

How did you make money in the first couple of months and how long did it take until you made money with your Youtube channel?
It took about a year until I got the first paycheck from Youtube. You must make more than $100 before they even bother sending you any money, and that really took forever.

Youtube has only become a viable source of income after I made the video that went viral. So, it was about two years that I wasn't making any money with it. I think it's normal that when you do something unique, it takes time for it to pick up.

What do your work days and your collaborations usually look like?
I'm involved in 15 different projects at the moment and I'm trying really, and I mean really, hard to stay organized. Usually, I'm waiting for people to send me angry emails because I didn't respond to them.

I've learned that if you have a day job, you need one that's flexible. Often, I have to leave around lunch because I've scheduled shootings in the afternoon. I also write for different blogs, like hellogiggles.com, brands, and magazines.

Essentially, I try to collaborate with as many people as possible. It's important to work with people that don't share your same exact audience. The more people I'm exposed to, the better. Usually I notice the biggest jump in subscribers after I've collaborated with someone else.

How much do you plan ahead?
I try to plan a full month ahead, but it feels like I get new emails every day where people ask me to do projects for them. Sometimes the deadline is as tight as the next day! I have to be open to these things. It's all very loosely planned, but I'm trying to make sure I know what the next month will look like, money and time wise.

But, as it is with freelancing, there are always ups and downs. Some months are dry and I always hope I have enough savings to get through the slower times.

How did you make money in the beginning?
I had a lot saved up when I went to freelance in March 2014. Also, I was still getting big checks from Youtube from the one video that went viral – that was about $ 500 to $ 600 each month.

In general, when you produce quality content online that makes you money, it's not like you have to produce something excellent each month. You just have to make sure people still watch what you uploaded a couple of months ago. The kind of content I produce is evergreen: there's always the possibility that someone finds the video in six months, shares it, and then it takes off again.

How do you represent yourself online and what platforms do you consider important?

Tumblr and Twitter are my favorite channels because that's where content has the best potential to go viral. And the way it can go viral would be impossible to achieve on a platform like Facebook or Instagram.

For example, if I post a makeup tutorial on Tumblr, I can tag it with #makeup and #beautyguru and all the people who are interested in that sort of content will find it, and maybe even share it.

The same goes for Twitter: you can take part in all these discussions and raise your voice. Also, the retweet function is just incredible! I feel like I'm on Twitter all the time, and the rest of the time, I'm trying to make everything else work. Somehow, I think people expect me to comment and be involved in the discussions.

— 70

The only way you can build an audience online is by being persistent and putting yourself out there regularly – and that requires you to start as soon as possible.

A big part of my job is to stay up-to-date on pop culture. Having something to say, being on social media is like its own project that helps me market myself. I think because I position myself as 'personality first', people are more willing to find me on other platforms and follow me there too.

I also have a website with a contact link, and surprisingly, people started using it. They usually refer to some other project where they've seen me involved and ask if I'd like to do something similar for their channels.

Could you give some practical tips to someone who wants to become a professional vlogger?

Start now! So many people wait to start a project until they think they have the perfect idea and have everything planned out. That's just not how the future works!

Now, with the internet, people are okay when things aren't perfect. At least as long as they're constantly getting better.

In the beginning, I tried to imitate people. I was trying to only publish content that was perfect. I wasted so much time!

The only way you can build an audience online is by being persistent and putting yourself out there regularly, and that requires you to start as soon as possible.

What I also think – and this is a hard one – is you shouldn't try to chase numbers. Your content shouldn't be driven by what has worked well in the past because it's never going to have the same effect again. Work on growing your art and doing things that interest you. That's how people will find that you're authentic and will start following your channel. ●

○ www.itsakilahobviously.com
○ twitter.com/akilahobviously

Go social

Facebook, Twitter, LinkedIn, Instagram, Pinterest, Youtube, Tumblr, Slideshare… You name it! There are so many social media platforms that it can feel a bit overwhelming to choose the right one for you and your business. The way businesses market their products and services on social media is changing every day, and so is the pricing, reach, and accuracy of various networks. I believe it's important to understand how a platform makes money to be able to decide how to best use it. Once a platform decides on how they will monetize their services, you'll be able to consider how to use the network for your business as cost efficiently as possible for the long run.

A couple of years ago, Facebook rolled out business pages and while they have been incredibly popular and very effective for small businesses, Facebook marketing has been getting increasingly expensive. Facebook profits from capping the reach of your page, which is why I'd recommend that if you decide to use Facebook to market your business to dedicate a budget: use Facebook for social ads or post on your personal page.

Facebook is a great tool to reach very specific target groups, as you can advertise to people based on their private situation. For example, if it's relevant to your business whether people have recently moved to a new country, graduated, got engaged (hello, wedding photographers, I'm looking at you), then Facebook might be the best tool for you to identify these people. You should definitely install the Ads Manager and check out what's possible.

Twitter is an incredibly handy tool to reach out to people you don't know. I've come to experience that Twitter is a very supportive community and everyone is incredibly helpful and open to meet up in person. I've been able to make really strong professional connections only by reacting to people's tweets and keeping in touch with them online. If you'd like to build a following on Twitter, you should focus on a specific topic.

Just like on Facebook, you can advertise on Twitter too. I'd recommend looking into Twitter ads if your products or services are related to big events because you can target specific hashtags which could feature your ads directly to an audience in need of them. On Facebook, you can easily advertise to people based on their personal situation, but on Twitter, it's more about their interests and topics of discussion people like to get involved in.

73

LinkedIn is denounced as an old-fashioned network, but nevertheless, it's worth a second look. Only recently, LinkedIn launched a feature that enables you to publish blog posts and share it with your professional connections, which helps you keep your contacts updated on what you're up to and vice versa. LinkedIn works like a social keyword database: the more keywords you have in your profile, the better. So, while I discouraged you to include what tools you use on your website, you should add them to your LinkedIn profile because many recruiters and headhunters look for freelancers on LinkedIn.

It's helpful to build your network on LinkedIn because the more connections you establish, the better you'll rank in people's searches when they are browsing for potential candidates for services they need. If you're a service provider, definitely include LinkedIn in your portfolio of social networks. Also, take the effort to add people as a connection you talked to after every networking event while they still remember your face.

Instagram is an incredibly popular network because it enables you to share images in an instant.

Broadly speaking, there are two kinds of Instagram accounts. The first group (which probably accounts for the majority of Instagramers) lets others peek into their personal lives. It's pictures of family, friends, snaps from occasional trips, and many, many selfies. Do you see what I see? These accounts are about their owners, which isn't of much interest to potential audiences, other than friends and relatives.

The second group is run by active community builders; these people provide a certain kind of service to their followers. Interests and services are very diverse of course, which is why these accounts vary in focus. They can be centered around anything, from personal styling to the Paleo diet. Active community builders tend to attract more followers because many of them are also involved in their community and are mentioned by fellow Instagram users.

If your business is visual, then Instagram is the perfect network to showcase your work and inspire people.

If you've ever wondered how successful Instagramers manage to make their images look so good, it's not because they use Instagram filters, but because they play around with editing and often use multiple apps to achieve the style they're after. Successful Instagramers have a style and follow through – thus, the followers know what they've subscribed to: it matches their taste and interest.

What should also be said is that not all Instagramers shoot their images with a smartphone. Some use a DSLR camera and then edit the image on their smartphone, but there are also many successful Instagramers who use their smartphones only. Here are some of the apps successful Instagramers use:

- ▸ **Snapseed** allows you to alter the brightness, ambience, and contrast, helps you straighten an image, crop it, and lets you do it all selectively to influence the depth of the image
- ▸ **VSCO** has a selection of beautiful filters. Some of them

are free, some are paid

- ▸ **SKRWT** helps you get straight lines. Great app for architects and minimalists
- ▸ **Retouch** enables you to get rid of stains, plugs, and all the other details that disturb your image
- ▸ **AntiCrop** helps you in the very tricky moment when you don't want to cut parts of your image away, but to make it Instagram-ready, you must make it into a square; AntiCrop stretches the background
- ▸ **Typographer** is a handy tool to add beautiful fonts to your image

75

If you're running an ecommerce business, then the platform of your choice should be the visual, bookmarking network: **Pinterest**. Most "pins" link to websites and often, these websites are shops. It's easy for users to click through to the image's source and buy the product. If you offer products or services of a visual nature and are able to distribute globally, then Pinterest is definitely your platform!

Youtube is the place to share how-to videos and short, sketch comedy shows. Remember Akilah?

Tumblr is a re-blogging tool and some really cool posts can go viral more easily on Tumblr than any other platform. It's fast and visual, so you should definitely upload beautiful images that catch people's attention immediately. Tumblr is popular amongst designers, illustrators, photographers, and many teens.

Slideshare is great for people who work in marketing and advertising. Just as the name already says, Slideshare is a tool to share your slides. If your work is not visual, then please give Slideshare a go because thinking in slides will help you visualize your content and will make it easier for people to digest. You can use Keynote, PowerPoint, Slides.com, or HaikuDeck to present your content and share it with fellow marketing professionals.

There are, of course, several other platforms, such as Behance for designers, GitHub for developers, Contently for writers, and so many more, but whichever platform you want to use to share your work, try to be consistent and open about your processes. As I have already said before, **share your work and share it often.** ◆

Gwen Boon

FASHION STORE OWNER, UTRECHT

"When something exceptional happens in a smaller city, everyone comes to check it out!" All too often, people feel discouraged starting their own business just because they don't live in a big city. Gwen believes that calling Utrecht her home was one of the reasons why her company became successful. Gwen shares her experiences with building a concept store that is more than just a fashion outlet. What she built is a brand and an indispensable part of the creative community in her area.

What did you study and why?
I studied arts and economics at the arts academy in Utrecht. I was always interested in business, I just wanted to specialize and do business in a creative area.

What happened between your university diploma and your current career?
After I graduated, I stayed at a gift shop where I had worked since high school. I knew I wanted to become my own boss eventually, so I was already on the lookout for ideas when I realized that there was not one good fashion store in Utrecht. Whenever I wanted new clothes, I had to go somewhere else.

I started working on a business plan for a concept store and told everyone that I was planning to open a fashion store in Utrecht. I was so excited about my plans that one day, my boss at work said he wanted to get involved. Literally, three months later I had my own store!

I never thought my boss would become a potential investor. I was just openly sharing my story and he really liked my idea and as he said, he had been in retail for a few decades and wanted to support a young entrepreneur.

What were the first steps you took to be able to open your own store?
I spent about four months working on my business plan. From the moment the investor joined me and we found a space close to the

centre, it only took about three months until we opened the doors. My investor found the space. We checked it out and there was a great café next door, so I thought I'd get some passing trade. The shop owner had about ten different applicants, so I was lucky to be the chosen one.

Then, I convinced two of my friends to help me create the brand and the interior design. All my friends helped out: we made a great deal of the furnishing ourselves and bought some additional displays from local carpenters.

Next, I had to decide what brands I wanted to sell. My intuition told me to look at the brands in my closet and contact them. While I was researching brands similar to the ones I already owned, I came across a list on the internet and used it.

— 80

There wasn't much planning involved. I just wrote them an email detailing what I planned, told them about the brands that already confirmed to work with me, and that was about it. I booked a trip to Copenhagen to meet as many designers in person as possible. I was very late in the year because usually, you place your orders in January and I placed mine in June, so I only received their excess stock but that was enough for me to start.

I managed to organize a collaboration with Wood Wood. I proposed a PopUp store to introduce their brand to the city and they provided me with their entire collection. We were able to move into our shop before we had

> When you do something new in a small city, everyone comes to check it out and word spreads much faster. It's easier to stand out.

any stock to sell. So when Wood Wood agreed to collaborate, it really felt like everything fell into place because we were able to try out different processes before we opened for real.

For the Wood Wood collaboration, we made the entire interior out of cardboard boxes. It was highly improvised, but being able to see how things evolved really helped us create the right kind of store.

How much budget did you have to start with?

I wrote a business plan where I initiated 100K, but then I only had 70K and to be honest, I am still recovering from having 30K less than planned.

In my business plan I had a buffer, which I eventually didn't have in reality, so when the bills started coming in, I had to make money straightaway to be able to pay my suppliers.

However, I couldn't pay everyone. Instead, I decided to have an open conversation with the different fashion brands and asked whether it was possible for me to pay them back later. The smaller brands, the beginners, were very supportive. I now know that without them, I wouldn't have a business today.

81

How important is it to be on a street where there are other shops with a similar concept?

I think it's really important. Other stores might be considered competition, but they attract more customers who will shop wherever they find something they really like. There's always going to be traffic around the area, which ultimately benefits everyone.

I was really lucky to have my store right next to Village Coffee & Music, which is a really popular indie café here in Utrecht.

How did you spread the word in the beginning?

In the beginning, mostly friends came and brought their friends who then referred Klijs & Boon to their friends: it was basically word-of-mouth.

What helped too was the PopUp store with Wood Wood. So many blogs wrote about it and even today, when you google 'Wood Wood Holland,' Klijs & Boon still comes up in the Google results.

People knew about the store very quickly. I think that's really an advantage when you do something new in a small city: everyone comes to check it out and word spreads much faster. It's easier to stand out.

When we first started, I invited all my friends to 'like' the Klijs & Boon Facebook page and when we had our Wood Wood event, we put up 'Like us on Facebook' signs on the walls. Luckily, our strategy snowballed.

How much stock should one start with?

I started with a lot of stock because if you have enough stock, you can become more profitable. I believe that it's better to have too much than too little because when people enter your store and there isn't much there to see, they probably won't come back.

When you start with € 30,000 worth of stock, you can make a decent profit. If you have less than that, it will be hard for you to make money. You do have to take a risk and start big if you really want to build a viable business.

Whatever you don't manage to sell at the end, you can sell in sales. After three years of running my own business, I have a stable and consistent amount of stock, which means that the number of boxes in my storage and shop roughly remains the same.

What do you consider the everyday difficulties of running a shop?

One of the main challenges is being able to multitask. I have to do the administration and marketing, I have to think of concepts for future projects, and, of course, I have to be there for the customers who come in. I enjoy all of it, but sometimes it would be helpful if someone would take care of the customers from time to time for me to be able to concentrate on future marketing initiatives.

I've always had people helping me out. In the beginning, I paid my friends by giving them vouchers. At some point, my accountant said that I couldn't give friends discounts as payment for working for me. I had to pay people properly. In that moment, I realized my business was growing up.

When I had to hire my first employee, I received 50 applications within one week. I chose ten that I would interview personally. I wanted to take the time to do everything right. I needed someone who could be in the shop when I was out taking care of errands and someone who would be able to join me for trips to Copenhangen. I basically needed someone I could fully trust. I think I made the right choice because she has been with me now for almost two years.

What do you do to grow the brand image of Klijs & Boon? How do you represent your brand online?

On one hand, I do everything I can for my customers to feel comfortable when they enter the door. I believe that it's part of my job to make their day better than it was before they stepped into my store.

Now that the shop's a little more established, I really try to come up with small projects and collaborate with other designers and entrepreneurs. For example, we've recently kicked off a collaboration where we feature different designers every month. Another one of our initiatives was a small collection of surprise packages we made for Christmas. We made 30 packages to test the concept and based on how well they sell and what the feedback is, we will make more next year.

I'm always trying to test every concept I come up with to make sure I don't invest too much money in something people aren't interested in. We also have events every other month. Some of them are sales events, which I always try to make fun because

83

> But you can't just write things down, you have to actually do what you write down.

they're such an essential aspect of running a fashion business.

Online, Klijs & Boon is on Facebook and we also have our own website. It used to be an online shop, but because running an online store is a whole business on its own, we've decided to drop it and only focus on in-store sales. Having an online market is not a priority of mine at this point in time.

Could you give some practical tips to someone who wants to open a store?

Surround yourself with people who want to help and don't hesitate to ask them for help when you need it. You can't do everything yourself. When I first started, I wrote many to-do lists. But you can't just write things down, you have to actually do what you write down.

In the beginning, I made a mistake that cost me € 20,000 because I bought too much stock from one brand, so be careful how you choose sizes and know what styles sell in your area. If you can, do a trial and see what sizes people buy most. I, for example, ordered too many mediums. But every shop is different, so base your decision on the feedback of your customers who come to your store.   ●

○ www.klijsenboon.nl
○ instagram.com/gwenboon

Gwen Boon • Fashion Store Owner, Utrecht

Network yourself up

My first question has always been, "How do people find clients?" There is a lot of competition out there, so I've always wondered what the secret was between the people who are always busy and the people who struggle to find work. I've finally figured out that the answer is this: people who are more successful are excellent networkers.

So, how does one become an excellent networker? And what does networking mean anyway?

If you think there is a secret to networking, I'm going disappoint you. There is no special way to approach people, nor are there general tactics to help break the ice between you and a stranger.

I personally believe that networking is a mind-set where you have a genuine interest in other people's work. You are willing to help them whenever they need your advice, resources, or a bridge to the people they want to meet. What I think also helps is the knowledge and appeal that you have something to give, just as the person who you're about to approach has something they can offer you or help you with. You are equals!

One of my strongest beliefs is there are no hierarchies between people. You are a human. The other person is a human. They have as much respect for you as you have for them. If not, they're not worth your time.

Generally speaking, there are two ways to meet new people: networking events and conferences or approaching people directly via social networks – the easier one.

The best way to find out about networking events in your area is meetup.com and eventbrite.com. It's easy to do a keyword search and find a group of people with common interests. If you can't find any events there, you might want to look up events at coworking spaces in your area. My favorite events are hosted by PechaKucha, TedX, and Creative Mornings. Also, gallery and store openings are the perfect places to meet people and potential clients. In case you live in a small town, you could start a monthly meetup yourself.

The other way to meet people who you'd like to have in your network is to approach them online. I prefer to use Twitter or Instagram to approach people I don't know. Mostly, it's enough to just say, "Could we have a coffee sometime next week?" If you feel uncomfortable about it, ask someone to introduce you to the person you want to meet yourself.

When you meet with others, always offer your assistance. People might not need your help immediately, but it's always good to let them know what you can provide and how they should best approach you. If someone approaches you, ask them clearly how you could help them and also, as Diana said, let people know you're available for projects.

Everyone needs a little help from time to time. Don't be afraid to pay favors forward. Make it clear to people that it's in your general interest to assist them on their way up. Don't ask for favors in return; treat your network as a favor network. Lend out your hand to someone and trust that they will lend theirs to someone else; eventually, someone will help you too.

In some professions, networking is the key that opens the doors, so being outgoing really helps. Here's Saba's story that might give you some clues on where to start. ◆

87

Saba Tark

FASHION DESIGNER, AMSTERDAM

In 2014, Saba's first Haute Couture collection was exhibited at the Centraal Museum Utrecht, and parts of the collection were bought for the museum's archives. Saba specializes in complex weaving techniques and likes to develop new ways to use textiles, which is characteristic for her collections. She speaks about the struggles of the fashion world in her interview, and also how she markets herself to collaborate and work with big industry names.

What did you study and why?

I studied fashion and textile design. Fashion has always been very present in our family, so it felt natural to follow the path.

What happened between your university diploma and your current career?

I have learned to understand that what they teach you at the academy doesn't have much in common with how it really works in the industry: you get more or less the opposite message. At the academy, they teach you to be creative and they make you believe that creativity is your most important asset, but what they don't tell you is that everything is restricted by money. You must understand how to do business and deal with the finances.

I've never been interested in commercial fashion. During my studies, I had the chance to intern with Iris van Herpen, Jan Taminiau, Lidewij Edelkoort, or Viktor & Rolf. You'd think that money doesn't play a role when you work in the Haute Couture branch, but my assumptions were proven wrong. I'm still trying to find a balance between creativity and monetizing my designs.

When I worked with Viktor & Rolf, I started as an unpaid intern before they offered me a real position. It was good, but I missed having the freedom to be creative and develop my skills on my own terms. I only stayed there for a couple of months.

How did you manage to get an internship with such prestigious brands?

I got involved with Fashionclash during my studies, which is an international platform that helps upcoming designers, and that gave me access to their mailing list.

In one of their emails, they announced that Jan Taminiau was looking for students to help him with his latest collection. Although it wasn't much money, the internship was paid. It really helped me understand how garments are made and what it means to take responsibility for their production.

You should always look for organizations that help young designers because they're the ones to hear first when there is an internship or a job available.

I also think that it matters where you study because designers often approach their former academies when they look for interns.

What were the first steps to starting your own fashion label?

I started looking for funding and awards and applied for them with the collection I made for my graduation. You really have to know how you'll finance your collection before you do anything else because it's impossible to make something outstanding without having any money.

I applied and received funding from the Dutch government that enabled me to create my first collection, *The Nomads of the World*.

The application process is a lot of work, but it pays off to take the time and actually do it. If you're only starting out, it's very unlikely you'll find an investor without any kind of leverage.

What you have to keep in the back of your mind is that as a small designer, you have to look for collaborators in your area. That will probably be more expensive than if you'd have everything produced in China, so try not to compete with mainstream fashion houses. Make something different.

I organized a show at Fashionclash and I was lucky because the people who run the Centraal Museum in Utrecht were sitting in the audience. About three weeks after the show, they reached out to me and asked if I would be interested in exhibiting my pieces at the museum.

They heard that I was nominated for the *Frans Molenaar Haute Couture Prize 2014*, which was a name that gave me additional leverage, and because they were looking for someone to do a solo exhibition, I decided to quit my job with Viktor & Rolf to be able to fully focus on this new challenge.

They bought half of my collection, which financed almost all of my spendings, but so far I haven't made any profit with my collection.

How much money did you have for your first collection?

I received € 10,000 in funding and I had some savings, so all in all, I had € 20,000 to start with. My first collection was entirely handwoven and I had all my shoes custom made too. I talked to a lot of specialists and even collaborated with a professor and his students from the technical university in Eindhoven.

I didn't really want to make compromises, so I made a collection I could be truly proud of. *The Nomads of the World* consists of seven garments, including custom made shoes.

The key really was that I reached out to the right people who helped me materialize my vision. I went to a lot of exhibitions and industry fairs and tried to create a network of people I admired for their work.

You must understand how to do business and deal with the finances.

I believe that it is important to be at as many events as possible, or at least as many events as actually possible, given you still have to produce good work. You must make sure you are to be seen and talked about; have a story and a concept. There is a lot of competition out there, so getting to know the right people really helps.

Does it help that you have blue hair?

No, I wouldn't say. It seems that people think I'm not that serious about what I do.

How do you represent yourself online? What platforms do you consider important?

Facebook really helped me get started. Every time I was looking for someone or something, I asked on Facebook.

Only recently I got a PR agency to help me promote my fashion. I think you really need one because every time a stylist looks for interesting pieces, they only approach agencies. You might get lucky and maybe a stylist who works for someone famous picks your garment, and then you'll receive a lot of press and people will know about your brand. The only thing many people underestimate is that this doesn't pay you a cent. It might be Lady Gaga or Kim Kardashian who wore your pieces, but you won't see any money from it. They don't buy the fashion, they lend it from PR agencies.

I'm really proud to work with my agency. We were able to find an agreement so I could eventually afford them. Generally speaking, people are really helpful and supportive when you share your vision with them and when they see that there is potential!

> The key was that I reached out to the right people who then helped me materialize my vision.

How do you market yourself and your fashion?

I have a very personal approach, so I go to a lot of exhibitions and events and talk to people. I give them my business card and I hope they follow up. Not everyone can afford my garments, so I'm working on a design system that would allow me to create the way I want to create, but will allow me to produce more affordable garments to broaden access to a wider audience of fashion lovers.

How do you make money?

Because the museum bought my garments, I have enough capital to create a second collection. I'm working towards the fashion week in the summer. I'm redefining the strategy and thinking of how I could reach new audiences, such as women in the Middle East, that would allow me to create the kind of fashion I want to be associated with.

Currently, I don't make any money. I'm giving myself time to re-evaluate whether I want to focus on my label or join another designer after I've created the next collection. So, I plan six months ahead.

Could you give some practical tips to someone who wants to become a fashion designer?

Don't expect to learn everything at the academy. You have to make a lot of effort to learn as many techniques as possible and there just isn't enough time to teach you that in four years.

93

Read fashion books and go to fashion shows. Network! And really take time to find awards or fundings you could apply to and are eligible for. I guess Google is your best friend! ●

○ www.sabatark.com
○ instagram.com/sabatark

Stand out

Generally speaking, there are three ways to spread the word about your business: treat your customers remarkably well and have them tell their family and friends about your business for you, pay for PR, or pursue something outstanding, such as collaborating with other great people or organizing memorable events.

Of course, it's always easier said than done and as Gwen said, it's probably easier to stand out in a small city than in a big city, but doing things differently helps.

The easiest way to find inspiration for how to make your business stand out is by looking at other branches or countries and become inspired from them. Ask a friend who goes on holidays to bring you back a local magazine you could learn from. Talk to people you know and admire and ask them if they'd like to do a project together with you. Plant the seed, that you want to make something outstanding, and bring in as many heads as possible and people will bring their ideas to you.

Good PR takes time; you need to identify the journalists who are interested in your matters and find out their contact details. Also, it pays off to build personal relationships, so if you have a chance to meet them in person, do it. Journalists and bloggers are busy because they get a lot of emails every day, so try reaching out to them via Twitter to bypass an overcrowded email inbox. If you'd like to send a press release, pull out several of the most newsworthy items and put them into a short email with the release pasted into the body of the email below. Journalists are often deterred by large email attachments and today's filters can often assign such emails as "junk." If all else fails, try to call or invite them to an event.

Take into account that while formal press releases still have a purpose, there are many other ways to achieve press. The field of content marketing is expanding rapidly and is a great way to engage customers without overtly conveying a sales mentality. Ask yourself if there is a particular subject for which your brand might be viewed as "an expert" by the media. Seek to create buzzworthy lists, image galleries, or even infographics to make your brand be seen as a leader in its respective field.

Here's Cristiana's story for the inspiration you may need when starting your new business endeavor. ◆

95

Cristiana Ventura

FASHION DESIGNER, SAO PAULO

If you think it's impossible to start a fashion business with just € 1,300 in your pocket, then it's about time you met Cristiana. She is a party girl and usually the last one to go home in the morning, but don't try to underestimate this gal. She's a hardworking business woman with focus and dedication.

She started her fashion brand, Hoxton, at the age of 25 and has been rocking the roofs and streets of Sao Paulo ever since. Her fashion, her colourful outfits, and her makeup are a way for her to express her feelings, which is why her outfits never turn dull. Here, she shares her insights on how to build a successful business literally from scratch and how to handle PR effectively.

97

What did you study and why?

Since I was a little girl, I was designing and making clothes for my Barbies. Fashion was the only thing I wanted to do in life, so I studied fashion. I attended ESMOD and then moved to London where I studied at Central Saint Martins with a major in conceptual fashion.

What happened between your university diploma and your current career?

I'd say: 'London happened!' Being so far away from Brazil changed my perspective on how I saw the world.

After finishing my studies at ESMOD, I got a job offer to work with a famous designer here in Brazil, but the paycheck was so ridiculously small that it didn't feel worth my time and efforts just to have their name on my resumé. I decided to continue studying instead, so I moved to London; the city of my childhood dreams.

While studying at Central Saint Martins, I got to know the people at Basso and Brooke and started working for them. That literally opened my mind and revolutionized my thinking.

I realized that what I really wanted was to have my own brand. Everyone in my family is an entrepreneur, so it felt natural to me to start my own business. Back then, I just didn't feel like I was ready yet. When it was time for me to return to Brazil, I started working for a really cool brand called NEON.

I enjoyed working there, but the salary wasn't enough for me to save up. If I wanted to start my own brand, I had to move on and get a better paying position. I started working for a company less 'cool,' but they paid much more. I worked there for about six or seven months.

Then in 2008, the next chance to go to London came along, which was right at the peak of the financial crisis. The city was grey, the people were grey, and I thought to myself, 'This is not what I've signed up for.' It was time to go home!

More than ever, this was the chance to start my own business, but I was still afraid to do it full-time. I freelanced with some companies and very slowly began to cut back my working hours to focus on my own brand. A good friend of mine took me aside and said that if I really wanted to make something out of my brand, I had to commit to it full-time.

My friends and family, everyone around me, kept urging that it was time for me to start my own company. They were very supportive and kept saying that I wasn't going to be happy working for someone else, doing things I wasn't necessarily keen on doing. Of course, that doesn't mean I'm now only doing things I love; I still have to tolerate Excel sheets from time to time. It's just that running your own business is overall very satisfying.

What were your first steps to start your own fashion brand?

I bought fabrics and negotiated with the retailer to pay them in rates; the first rate was due after 30 days and the second after 90 days. That gave me 30 days to produce and sell at least some of the garments. I knew my reputation was everything, so it really was my first priority to pay the rates on time.

I had about € 1,300 to start off my business. I used the money to pay the people – freelance pattern cutters and seamstresses – who helped me out. I started my business on an extremely tight budget, but I've learned that when you set yourself a goal and dedicate your time and thought to it, you'll reach it!

People in my surroundings were very supportive. My first customers were mostly friends and family and then a little later, friends of friends. The great thing about fashion is that when someone sees clothes they like, it's very likely they'll ask about the brand's name. People started adding me on Facebook and that's basically how it all started.

How did you make money in the first couple of months?

That was hard! I had some savings and because I was still working for another company two days a week in the very beginning, I was able to survive. As long as I had a roof above my head, I was okay. I learned that you can stretch money and buy really cheap groceries. As long as you can pay your bills on time, you're fine! I didn't have to pay rent and that helped a lot.

99

To cut costs, I first started working from home. It was a mess! I worked from home for almost two and a half collections. After about nine months, I was able to rent a small room where I could show my outfits. I signed a

> As long as I had a roof above my head, I was okay. I learned that you can stretch money and buy cheap groceries.

contract for a year, and only after this year I was able to rent a small shop, which I have under contract for three years.

What was your process to deal with budgets and pricing?

I'm a very visual person, so I put up large sheets of paper all over my apartment and wrote everything down: how much all my expenses were, when I had to pay for them, and how much I could spend on fabrics and accessories. I wrote down all my deadlines; I literally surrounded myself by my own accountancy.

When things became tight, I went freelancing. Sometimes once a week, sometimes once a month.

I eventually had some profit, which was slightly bigger than what I expected. I invested the money back to my company and started working on my second collection.

Do you have investors for your brand?

After two years of being in business, someone approached me because they wanted to invest in my company. They knew me and my work and their dream was to work in fashion. They didn't just put money in my business, they became my partner, which eventually didn't work out. I need my creative freedom. I like working on my own and I like to have the last word.

What I've learned from the failed collaboration is that if I would ever consider getting someone else onboard, I would look for someone who has a very different skillset; someone who enjoys dealing with the finances and the administrative part of running a business and doesn't interfere with my ideas when it comes to the creative direction of *Hoxton*.

At some point, I felt like I was a slave to my own company. I had to be in the shop all the time and my business has since evolved into a very commercial route. Now I have the chance to build a business I actually want to work for. My plan is to give crowdfunding a go, look for partners in retail, and I'm working on building an online shop. Also, for the first time in years, I'm going to take a few months off!

Save up! You have to have money, to spend money, to make money!

Now that you are rebuilding your business, is there something that scares you?

Of course! One of my biggest fears is not being able to handle the pressure. I know that if we really want something, we can work 20 hours to solve our challenges. However, my business is no longer just about me and my needs: I have employees and suppliers and it's my responsibility that they can feed their families. So it's not a fear, but a challenge. It's a challenge to be taken seriously!

How do you market your fashion?

I love to do my own marketing. I have a PR agency and they stock my garments and provide them to magazines for shootings if needed.

I really enjoy experiential marketing, so I do it myself. I love throwing rooftop parties above my shop. One of my partners is Jack Daniel's, so they supply me with drinks and it's great fun to work with them. The collaboration has helped me attract people who would usually never stumble upon my business. My brand was featured in many of Brazil's women's magazines and I didn't have to pay a cent for that to happen.

How do you represent yourself online? What platforms do you consider important?

I'm a big fan of Facebook and Instagram. Although, I can't say there is a strategy behind how I use it. If people follow me, great. If not, that's also great.

I know that even if people don't like and favorite my images, they still see them. Often enough when people approach me, they refer to something I posted online. So even if I don't see an image is popular online per se, I know it still serves a purpose.

Could you give some practical tips to someone who wants to become a fashion designer?

Read. Read at least one book every month. And don't just read books that are fashion related. Be open to new insights and experiences. Go to museums and explore your surroundings. Travel as much as your budget allows you to. Go and live abroad, leave home, wherever home is to you, and soak in as much as you can!

And to give you some practical tips: save up! Start saving up as soon as you can because you'll need the money. You have to have money, to spend money, to make money! ●

○ www.hoxton.com.br
○ instagram.com/cristiana_ventura

Join a collective

Imagine yourself in a loud, noisy bar. You're having a hard time hearing the one person you're trying to have a conversation with. You don't know most of the people there, you don't know who to talk to, and you don't know how you could even approach them. This can be a very stressful social situation indeed, so chances are high you might not enjoy socializing as much as others do, and that's okay. But as daunting as networking may seem, it can also be downright enjoyable. When you match it to your strengths and interests, there truly are ways to build a network while doing what you enjoy doing, and not have social anxiety in the process.

One way to build a network is by volunteering with an organization you admire in your community. If you're a fan of a particular cause or know of an organization whose work you like and support, then you should get involved! That's exactly where the people are that you want to meet.

If volunteering isn't an option, the easiest way to network on your own terms is by finding or starting a group of people with a shared interest who can work and support each other. I'm talking about professional collectives: groups of people with a common interest who recommend one another.

Finding a group of people with a shared interest but possess different styles is essential, especially in the creative industries. If a potential client expresses interest working with i.e. a blogger, but they don't quite like the style or the blogger doesn't think it's a good fit for them, they can refer the client to someone else in the collective and the client "doesn't get lost." Having a collective is like building your own referral network. Lea and Aisha (both stories are yet to come), co-founded collectives: Lea is a travel blogger and she collaborates with other travel bloggers who all specialize on different aspects of a journey, and Aisha is a comic designer and an illustrator who has a collective of fellow illustrators that help her find work as much as she helps them.

Now, enjoy Lea's story to learn more about the dynamic of her collective. ◆ 103 —

Lea Hajner

TRAVEL BLOGGER, INNSBRUCK

When you want to become a travel blogger, you need a niche. Lea found hers by moving out of the city and into the Austrian Alps. She started a blog with a focus on nature and travel outside of busy city life called *Escape Town*. In her interview, she discusses how she transformed her love for travel into a viable career and the importance of networking; building relationships with people in your industry and also with those who could one day hire you for projects and assignments.

What did you study and why?

When I was in high school, my German teacher encouraged me to become a writer, so that was the seed that planted the idea. I was lucky enough to get into journalism in Vienna and graduated with a major in media management.

What happened between your university diploma and your current career?

During my last year at university, I did an internship at a startup. This opened up the whole startup and entrepreneurial scene in Vienna for me. After my internship, I went traveling on my own and spent eight months living out of my backpack, getting to know 12 different countries around the world. I've always loved traveling and wanted to experience different cultures, gather new views on life, and become inspired. After my return, one of the people I previously worked with asked me to join their recently founded travel guide platform, Tripwolf, and become their PR and social media manager. After three years working with them, I relocated to Innsbruck for personal reasons.

In the beginning, I worked remotely, but I missed having my work colleagues in the same room. Also, I already had some ideas and was just waiting for the right moment. All of the sudden, it felt right to start something new on my own.

What were your first steps to become a travel blogger?

Part of my job at Tripwolf was to manage guest authors who contributed to our blog and take care of the social media channels. In 2010, I was sent to the first ever travel blogger conference in Europe. This is where I met people who actually made a living out of traveling and writing about it. It sounded like a dream job and for the first time, I realized that I could combine my passion for traveling and my background in PR and writing to make a career out of it.

About a year later, I started my own travel blog. Starting a blog wasn't something I did spontaneously. I used to have one during university, but this was my chance to make a fresh start. I was planning how to do it for months. From the start, I didn't accept any banners or sneaky ads. All I have on my blog are sponsored blog posts, marked as such. However, it's not the blog where my salary comes from, but it's from the content, which I produce for other companies and media houses.

You need a good camera, a smartphone, and a laptop. Of course, it's not just about owning devices. You must know how to use them too.

Sometimes I get sent to places just to write and produce content for corporate channels. To give you an example, I recently collaborated with the Filipino tourist board. They sent me to travel around the country and write about it. The posts I wrote will be used for the German website to encourage tourism. In 2013, I also worked with Lufthansa. Together with a blogger colleague, they sent us on a trip to Hamburg to produce a small campaign for their Instagram channel.

How do your clients find you?

I'd say it's mostly because of my extensive networking. I've known the people, who are now my clients, for years. I often get emails asking me what I'm up to these days and whether I have time to work on a project.

106

Sometimes people ask me because they googled 'travel blogger' and liked my website. I really believe that it's important to have a network and an expressive online presence.

Another thing I can recommend is to create a collective with people in your field, or one closely related to it. I'm part of the Reiseblogger Kollektiv, which is a group of travel bloggers who decided to collaborate. We are not a company, but we all have our own niche. If, for example, someone receives an invitation but they can't make it or they're approached by someone who's looking for a specific type of content that doesn't fit their personality, they'll pass it on or refer someone else in the group. It's been very beneficial for all of us and I'm glad to be working with such great people.

107 —

What are the tools a travel blogger needs?

You need a good camera, a smartphone, and a laptop. Of course, it's not just about owning devices. You must know how to use them too, a fact that's widely underestimated by DSLR owners all across the world. But seriously, it's a mixture between your tools and your skills.

As a travel blogger, I'm a one-woman business, so knowing a bit of everything helps: some knowledge about SEO, some about HTML, and some about how to setup a website. Of course, you can ask people to help you, but it's valuable to at least know how to communicate your needs.

Don't forget you also need a network! Go to conferences and industry events to talk to everyone about what you do. Those are your tools as well.

How do you organize your day-to-day?

My days start with checking my emails and Instagram, then I go from there. Sometimes, I spend four days in front of the computer and type from the morning until late at night, or I might have a lazy week and go snowboarding and only work for a couple of hours. It depends on the deadlines. I like to get things done early to have a buffer. I don't like delivering assignments at the last minute.

How did you make money in the first couple of months?

I found a client who wanted to work with me before I quit my job. It was a project for six months, so I knew where the money would be coming from in the beginning. From then on, things just started happening.

When I first started, it was all trial and error, but I knew that if things didn't work out that I could always look for another job. I gave myself a year to make things work, and I did!

In the first year, I underestimated accounting and regularly forgot to collect the receipts. A beginner's mistake, you might call it. So yes, my biggest challenge wasn't the writing or finding clients, it was organizing myself and working out the business side.

Another struggle I had was finding the right price for my services. I quickly learned how to talk to people who wanted me to work for free, but I often underrated how much I needed to charge. Sometimes you really want to work with someone, so you offer your services below what you need to make a living. You really have to remind yourself that the payment must pay for rent and daily needs. Finding your price is not easy, but talking to more experienced colleagues is always a big help.

> A beginner's mistake: In the first year, I underestimated accounting and regularly forgot to collect the receipts.

How do you represent yourself online? What platforms do you use?

I obviously have my blog where I publish content several times a week. I then spread my own content across my social media channels. Facebook is probably the most important one for me. I use it to stay connected with colleagues, as well as for promoting my articles. I have a Facebook page, which has grown steadily over the last few years.

And then, there's Instagram, which I love to use professionally and personally. I have a Twitter account, but for me, it's more a B2B channel. I also have a profile on Xing and LinkedIn to stay in touch with business contacts.

How much in advance do you plan? How many months in advance can you say you know what you'll be doing?

Last year, I almost always knew what projects were going to happen throughout the year. Now, I can't say what's going to happen next year just yet. I feel I can't really plan so much in advance, but I'm confident that there will always be work.

Could you give some practical tips to someone who wants to become a travel blogger?

Most of all, I think it's important to be passionate about travel. Remember that the job of a travel blogger isn't about hitting the road and also it's nothing like a constant vacation. Essentially, it's about extensive research, hours and hours spent on planes, trains, and buses, as well as almost the same amount of time spent in front of a computer, sorting through photos, and getting everyday things done. It's about writing, telling interesting stories, and providing something of unique value to your readers and eventually, to your clients. ●

○ www.escape-town.com
○ twitter.com/esctown

Test your ideas

Usually, when starting a project, we think of the big outcome we want to achieve as an end result and we tend to forget all the little steps that are necessary to lead us there. One of the hardest lessons you learn in design school is to prototype; to test your ideas. Before you design the entire building in a 3D program, you should make a rough paper prototype to test the dimensions to determine if your idea actually works before you invest a tremendous amount of time in something that, in the end, doesn't work. The same goes for almost any project you start: you need to test it before you've wasted your valuable time and money.

As I've already said in the beginning, having a business plan doesn't mean things are set in stone; it just means that you have an idea and know what to do to start executing. At the same time, having a business plan means you've put a price tag on every position and every task that's necessary to reach your big, celebratory outcome. Testing your idea, on the other hand, means that you'll have to find a solution to work around the price tag because it's very likely you don't have the amount of money that's needed just yet.

One of the most valuable things Anne said to me when I interviewed her was that to be able to think outside of the box, you must make the box very small and try to figure out a solution that fits within the small box. Your small box is where you are before you've invested any money. Every solution you can come up with now, within your small box, will help you create a project that's more unique, something Anne will explain in her story. But testing your ideas is not just a way for you to save money and make a concept that's unique; it will help you make the right decisions before you scale up. Running a test trial will help you to understand your customers better and it will help you decide what changes to make that you'll see are necessary. Why else do you think the popup concept exists? You can make popups for almost anything: restaurants, fashion stores, or galleries.

You've already read Gwen's story, but here's Anne's take on what she's learned from running a test trial. ◆

Anne Kjær Riechert

EVENT ORGANIZER, BERLIN

Born in Denmark and brought up in Norway, Anne is the driving force behind the *Berlin Peace Innovation Lab* in collaboration with the Stanford Peace Innovation Lab. She started the community and event series in 2013, and is now working on monetizing her side project to be able to focus on it full-time. If you face constraints that make you feel as if there is too much in your way to make your project a reality, this interview gives you the right stimulation not to give up!

What did you study and why?

I always thought I would become an international correspondent and I was aiming at studying journalism, but when I had to decide what to study, I came across a program in entrepreneurship and innovation management at a school called Kaospilot in Århus, Denmark. Everything I read about the school and its programs sounded exactly like me. I had to do it!

After I graduated, I worked as a consultant for Samsung Electronics. It was a good position; nevertheless, my ambitions were much higher than what seemed possible back then. I wanted to have more of a social impact. I wanted to drive change more efficiently, so I decided to go back to university to learn more about open innovation processes and peace building.

The option came up to study at ICU in Tokyo for my masters. It was a wild card, but I was already curious about social innovation in Asia. I didn't know much about corporate responsibility nor social entrepreneurship in Japan, but I thought, 'when else will I get the chance to live in Japan for two years?' so I went for it! The earthquake, tsunami, and nuclear disaster in Fukushima in 2011 coincided with my studies. In the end, it wasn't so much the university that shaped my interest in social impact, but rather the tremendous events I had lived through: they have had a real impact on my life and professional choices ever since.

I saw the importance of efficient collaboration and how technology can help us. When it's hard for people to find food and water, you suddenly realize how important collaboration is. Only a few were experts in nuclear radiation, but in a situation like this, you feel the need to understand as much as possible as quickly as possible. You are bombarded by an incredible amount of information from many different sources and only have a short time frame to reach a decision.

So, what happened between finishing your academic education and your current career?

I don't think I'm done studying. I think it's important to find a balance between theory and practice. I was offered to pursue a PhD program at Stanford, but I wasn't feeling ready at that time. Instead of jumping right into another academic program, I decided to move to Berlin to apply what I had learned during my masters. I offered to the representatives from Stanford to found a division of the Peace Innovation Lab in my new hometown. That was back in the autumn of 2012.

In Berlin, I joined Coca-Cola Germany in their corporate social responsibility department in a part-time position that left enough time for me to focus on my side projects, my 8-year-old youth empowerment movement 'Kids Have A Dream' and the 'Berlin Peace Innovation Lab.'

What were your first steps to establish an event series, like the Peace Innovation Lab, in Berlin?

I spent six months trying to figure out the right business model and find the right people to run the Peace Innovation Lab with. I deliberately wanted someone with a different skill set than mine; someone who had experience in technology and fundraising. I did find someone, but in the end, I realized that we weren't a very good fit. Instead of looking for someone else, I decided to continue with the project on my own.

There was no proof of concept, no proof if what I was working on would have any traction. I didn't know if people were interested and would come to the event. I decided to contact the representatives at Stanford and ask whether someone was available to come to Berlin and give a talk. Instead of planning, I started organizing the first actual event.

I had no budget to pay for a room, so I started looking for companies and organizations that shared the same values and found one to collaborate with: Betterplace.org, a social enterprise, would host our first event.

In the beginning, not having any budget or space felt like a constraint, but now I see it as one of our biggest advantages because it forced us to find new partners. Not having our own space helps us keep overheads at a minimum. Also, the longer you do something and do it well, the easier it becomes. Over the years, I've been building a large global network of people, which is something everyone should focus on.

115

To spread the word about the *Berlin Peace Innovation Lab*, we used meetup.com. The platform is very clever: after you create an event and fill out all the important details, come up with a good theme and a catchy description, then meetup. com informs their members who share your interest and live in the area about your venture. One and a half years later, there are more than 600 people in our network, which is about enough to have 50 attendees at every event.

> The longer you do something and do it well, the easier it becomes.

How much time do you spend organizing the Peace Innovation Lab?
I would say I need four full days to organize an event every month. It takes time to create a pipeline of interesting speakers. The workload always depends on the impact we want to create and the partners we want to work with.

Do you think someone without your academic background could run an event series like this?
Essentially, yes. Everyone can setup an event series on meetup.com and start from there.

The *Berlin Peace Innovation Lab* is, however, my creation. It has been created around my vision, but has been shaped organically over time based on the feedback from our partners and our community.

It's exciting that people with a vision now also have affordable technology to help them realize it. How people decide to use these digital tools is entirely up to them.

What is your vision for the event?

After one and a half years of organizing one to two events every month, I feel like it's time to take the next step and turn the *Berlin Peace Innovation Lab* into a sustainable business. I want to facilitate a knowledge exchange and bring great companies, universities, government, and civil society together to really have an impact on peace in the world; I'm aware that it is a very ambitious goal.

116

It's commendable to have social impact, but you really need to understand how to monetize your project to make it self-sustaining; to be able to scale up. My aim is to create a concept that is sharp and recognizable in its own right so it doesn't rely on the leverage of our Stanford association. I also want others to be able to copy the event in other cities.

When people ask me how to think outside of the box, I always say that they just have to make the box very small and figure out a solution that fits inside of the box.

We can increase our international impact if the events can be run without my presence, but run by people in other cities and other countries around the world. I have been thinking a lot about leadership and its meaning lately. I believe leadership is the ability to bring out the best in people, help them realize what their purpose is, and help them flourish without telling them what to do.

I have hired consultants to help me figure out the right business model and sharpen the concept. I would love to build an innovation agency based on the collective intelligence of our community and associated partners; an agency that is able to tackle the really big social and environmental challenges that our world is facing.

We've slowly started introducing money in different ways to see how it changes the dynamic of the group. We ask ourselves who should be the ones paying: should the attendees pay? Should the partners who host us pay a fee? Or should companies who propose a challenge be the ones paying? And how much should they pay? Money is closely connected to our perception of value. If it's free, many people won't regard it as valuable.

There truly are many directions we can take for the next step. Based on what the consultants propose and my mentors recommend, we'll start testing different directions. We need feedback and will improve based on actual experiences rather than build something based on market assumptions. I believe in co-creating with our customers and consumers to make sure our product fits what the market needs.

I'm carefully trying to build an organization that can exist independent of me. It matters to have a powerful founder story to tell, but I want people to focus less on the people involved and more on the good work that is being produced.

What do you think makes for an impactful event?

I believe it's the people in the room, but bringing interesting people together often isn't enough. The *Berlin Peace Innovation Lab* is a highly facilitated event and workshop. We always start with a team building energizer, followed by a 30 minute inspirational talk, then we split in small groups for discussions or brainstorms. In the end, all groups share their insights.

I have been to so many events where you have great minds in one room, but they end up drinking and talking to people they already know because no one gave them a common ground or a structured agenda to bring out the best in them.

We usually have drinks together after the Berlin Peace Innovation Lab as well. That is however, after we have all collaborated and know who would be interesting for us to talk to.

What happens with the outcomes of the workshops at the Peace Innovation Lab events?

The *Berlin Peace Innovation Lab* currently doesn't execute on any of the ideas. Our purpose is bringing good people together and giving them the opportunity to meet like-minded others who they could collaborate with and give them inspiration for the projects they're working on or want to work on in the future. Currently, we have invested solely in raising our social capital. The better our community does, the easier it is to communicate why we're doing what we're doing.

How do you personally represent yourself online and what platforms do you consider important?

For me personally, the most important channel has been Facebook. Not the Facebook page, which I created for the *Peace Innovation Lab*, but my private profile. I notice how important my personality is for the success of the projects I run. Everything I do online helps my projects gain traction, but I worry that people care more about my personal journey and less about the impact of the work I do.

For the event itself, the decision to represent us on meetup.com has helped immensely.

Could you give some practical tips to someone who wants to organize an impactful series of events?

With anything you do, start doing it now and learn along the way. Don't plan for months without having a proof of concept. With us, 50 people turned up at the first event, but even if it was just three people, that would have already been an indicator of how many people are interested. It would also be three people in the room to ask for feedback and to help you spread the word.

Restrictions are the best guides when you need to come up with a concept that stands out, and I think they can work to your advantage. When people ask me how to think outside of the box, I always say that they just have to make the box very small and figure out a solution that fits inside of the box. If you don't have space, money, or anything else you think you need, see it as a challenge to be solved, not a problem that makes you give up. ●

○ www.bit.ly/berlinpeaceinnovationlab
○ twitter.com/anneriechert

Get your business funded

Do you have a great idea, but no money to help you get started? In case you need funding to finance your tools or to keep you afloat while you focus on your project, then I might have some good news for you! As Maxie already mentioned, there are many organizations that are more than happy to help you finance your business idea as long as you deliver a business plan that's thorough and touches people.

In some countries, at least in Europe, the government offers support by paying upcoming entrepreneurs a remuneration for a couple of months for them to be able to focus on building their business. Talk to the labor office or to the chamber of commerce to find out whether your country offers such support.

If the country where you live doesn't offer any financial assistance, don't let this get you down! There are several organizations that provide grants to businesses when they believe in their vision. The main challenge is to find the right fund that supports businesses with a similar mission like yours.

To get your business funded, there are two obstacles: you need to find the right fund, which might take as long as the second step, establishing an impressive business plan. Most funds are country-specific or are, for example, given by the European Union. At this point, there isn't a single go-to website where all available fundings and grants would be listed, so you'll need to invest some of your time and research, or ask around within your personal network. The following are some of the funds Maxie recommended:

▸ The Global Social Entrepreneurship Competition (US)
▸ Sustainia100 (Global)
▸ Ben & Jerry's Join Our Core (EU)
▸ Future Impact Award (selected countries in Europe)

121

Different organizations support different types of businesses, so if your project doesn't get the support you hoped for, you've either picked the wrong organization or you need to put some extra work into your business plan to make proper modifications.

If you can't find the right funding that would help you get started or have a much bigger vision than what a state funding could potentially cover, you can either start a crowdfunding campaign on a platform, such as Kickstarter or IndieGoGo, or you might need to look for investors to support your business.

If you, like Gwen, are lucky to find an investor in your social circle by sharing your goals openly with the people around you, that's great! Unfortunately, not everyone has the same kind of luck and, as always, that's okay. There are a million ways to get to where you want to be, so it's just a matter of finding the right one.

It might be easier to look for investors in the so-called startup capitals of the world, such as London, Berlin, Tel Aviv, New York, or San Francisco. In startup hubs, there are many events that enable you to meet the right kind of people and connect to the startup ecosystem. Don't just look for people who can give you money and don't ask for money straight away; build relationships and talk to people who have already found investors for their businesses. Make friends and involve people in your process.

If you're new to the startup world and don't live in a city that has a flourishing scene, then it might be a good idea to go on a little research expedition.

Before you book a plane ticket somewhere, see what companies have their offices there. You might want to look on startup job boards to at least get the names of different companies. Once you find some thriving companies, don't hesitate to reach out and ask them for a coffee date. Most of the time, people are generous and will meet you for at least 20 minutes. Also, look for different startup meetings and events and don't hesitate to join. Meetup and Eventbrite are good platforms to find the kind of events you're looking for. Then, you should look for a coworking space in the city and book a table there for a couple of days. Coworking spaces usually run a series of startup meetups, so participate in as many as you can. In the next interview, Olga has shared some of her insights on how the startup scene works. ◆

123

Olga Steidl

STARTUP FOUNDER, BERLIN

At the age of 26, she was the Vice President of Yandex, a Russian search engine. Olga has built several businesses and helped upcoming startups with their products and growth marketing. Today, Olga works for Inbot App. Here, she speaks about choosing the right people to work with, hiring employees, investor relationships, and what she wishes someone told her before she became an entrepreneur.

What did you study and why?
I studied IT management and enjoyed it a lot. I now build enterprise systems, so retrospectively, it was the right choice.

What happened between your university diploma and your current career?
I first started working when I was 15. My mother noticed that I was bored, so she decided to help me get a job that would keep me occupied.

I was helping PhD students to digitize their dissertations even though I was young and didn't understand a word. Let me rephrase that: I understood the words, just not the context of what I was typing. The whole job didn't make much sense because I'm dyslexic, so it was challenging, but I was earning good money and had the opportunity to learn how to take responsibility for my own life. I stayed there for three years and then moved into a position where I was installing IT systems. It was a rather illogical step in my professional career, given I'm not an engineer, so I switched jobs again.

I decided I wanted to work for an up-and-coming beer company, which is funny because that also didn't make much sense: I don't drink alcohol. Then, when I was 20, I changed jobs again. I started working in a corporate environment, but quickly learned that I like things to move quickly and I like progression. I clearly wasn't the type to work in a corporate environment, so I changed jobs again and started working for a startup!

There, I saw what being 'burned out' really meant; when my boss started throwing potted plants at my colleagues, I knew it was time for me to get out of there and to do so as quickly as possible.

At this point, I've seen a lot and have learned what I don't want in my professional life. I knew I had to be more careful with my next step.

Then one day, someone who followed me on livejournal.com, a popular network in Russia, contacted me. They needed a marketing manager and he knew I was looking for work. I joined the company. At that time, there were 30 developers and I was their first marketing and business development hire. After six years with the company, we existed to Yandex. Suddenly, I was on the board of directors and became Yandex's Vice President. I was only 26. It was pretty cool, and I was young and arrogant. After we exited, I joined a venture fund and helped them with one of their startups. I moved to Berlin and worked on a couple of projects, helped out a few companies. I really liked one of the teams and when they asked me if I wanted to join their company, I said yes.

What made you decide you wanted to become an entrepreneur?
I hated my corporate job. I felt observed and micromanaged and I really don't like politics. I figured being an entrepreneur or finding a group of entrepreneurial people who trust you fully was the only way for me to be happy with my professional environment.

How does it work with money in the startup scene where companies aren't financially stable yet?
I worked with startups and I also co-founded some. What I've learned is that you must be prepared that your income really isn't predictable and also much lower than if you work for a corporation. It's important to stay flexible, and if you happen to get funding in the beginning, you must remember that the money won't be there forever. So yes, you must be ready to hustle!

As an entrepreneur, every decision you make, whether it's how many people you hire or how much your office furniture costs, you must be 100% sure it was the right way to spend money.

I'm not a fan of cool accelerators because teams get fancy offices, food, and all the goodies they can think of, and are then shocked when they're forced to downgrade once the program's over.

So, how does a startup founder budget their income?
There are good and bad startup founders. If you look at the stellar structure, you can see how big the founder's ego is: if a founder budgets themselves much higher than how they budget the rest of the team, then they value themselves more than everyone else. Such a startup will get into troubles and I'm not interested in working with them. If founders get the same salary as, let's say, the developers or a bit less, then you know these founders really want to make their businesses work. They understand where the money is really needed; those are the kind of startups I work with.

127

Could you explain how it works with funding in the startup world?
In terms of my current company, I think it was much easier to raise funding because all of us have a track record of past successes. Otherwise, it probably would have been impossible to raise 2.6 million in seed funding.

In general, it's much easier to find investors when you identify what type of company an investor's interested in. Don't approach them and ask for money straightaway. Try to build a relationship and involve them in your process, or maybe ask for advice. Also, try to build a relationship with the other companies they've invested in. They might ask what the teams in the companies they have invested in think about you and your business, and if they have never heard your name, you'll probably be off the table very quickly.

> Founder's ego: if a founder budgets themselves much higher than how they budget the rest of the team, then they value themselves more than everyone else.

What do you wish someone told you before you became an entrepreneur?

As an entrepreneur, your business is your toy and you often don't want to talk about or do anything else. But I've learned that you do need to understand that your business is not everything. You must find balance for yourself and try to spend quality time with friends and family. When your business falls apart, which can happen even to the smartest and most successful people, you'll need somewhere to go. Someone should have also told me that things take time. I make decisions fast and expect things to move at a fast pace too, but some things just need time and being patient has been my biggest challenge.

How do you choose people you work with?

I learned the hard way who to trust. I used to trust everyone immediately because I'm a trustworthy person, but then things happened where I felt betrayed. Now, I always try to spend as much time with a person as possible to get to know them before I decide to trust or work with them.

You might have a great relationship with someone, but unless you've worked with them before, you don't know their dynamic yet. Before I say 'yes' to a contract now, I try to work on something small with them, kind of as a trial run.

I've also learned that cooking can help me recognize who to work with. If a person micromanages me, I can determine that we won't work together well. If I have to manage them, it won't work either.

One thing that has proven successful in the last couple of years is before I start looking for people publicly, I look through my Evernote if I already have a suitable person in my network. Evernote is like my personal Wikipedia; that's where I have all my notes and also notes I make after I meet people, so if I ever need someone specific, I know where to look. And I screen for cultural fit of course! The person must have the same values as the team and they must be genuine. I refuse to work with a*sholes.

Another thing I've learned, and it's not necessarily about working with people, is the way I use Twitter. I like to create lists and whenever I need, for example, journalists to talk to, I'll probably have them in one of my Twitter lists. It makes it easier for me to reach out to contact them.

How did/do you convince people to trust you and your ability to build businesses at such a young age?

I've always had a really big ego. I thought I could do whatever I wanted and that I was clever enough to pull it off too.

I'm a skilled marketer, so I've learned to turn things around to change the perspective of how people look at an issue and how I should pitch it to them. I can adapt stories so people hear what they're eventually looking for. But, don't get me wrong, I'd never betray anyone. I want to be trusted, so I always hustle to accomplish what I promised.

I think that people trusted me for various reasons; partly because of my loud yelling that I could do anything! But then, people might have thought, 'This Olga's a cool kid and we should give her a chance.' Now I have references and a proven record of what I've accomplished.

What's also important to me is that I only use social media in a professional context. I don't like when people are able to know what's going on in my private life because they read it online.

For work, Facebook for example, really does miracles: you can look for something in the middle of the night and people will refer you to what or who you're looking for. I like @medium a lot and share many of my insights there. That also creates leverage.

Could you give some practical tips to someone who wants to build a viable business or found a startup?

First, don't hire a marketing person before you have a good product.

Hire a community manager, someone who will help you with user interviews and making a product that fits the market.

Most startups ask the wrong questions. If someone asks, 'If I give you this tool, would you do this and that?' That's literally the worst possible question to approach someone with. Instead, ask, 'How do you do it now and what's your biggest problem with it?'

Also, don't quit your day job until you have validation for your concept. You can start building a business while you work for someone else. And last but not least, be careful when you hire and always hire one person less than you think you need. Limited resources make people more creative! ●

○ www.linkedin.com/in/olgasteidl
○ twitter.com/olgasteidl

Olga Steidl • Startup Founder, Berlin

Be flexible

If starting a business or freelancing was easy, everyone would do it. The truth is, it's always risky because you never know if your business model will pick up or if your services are as needed as you hoped for when you first started. Also, there are jobs where at times, you'll hardly have work at all.

Many freelancers, when they first start out, don't have as many clients and thus, have lots of free time on their hands. Others can get extremely busy at times, and then they don't have much to do for a couple of weeks or even months. Regardless of which category you fall into, should you ever find yourself in a situation with less work, don't panic; instead, see this time as a chance to expand your portfolio and try out something new that keeps you on your toes.

When Lisa couldn't sell enough dresses to keep her business going, she started looking for a cheaper product to include in her online store. She made paper origami, which became more popular than the dresses she was producing when she first started her fashion business. Lisa now works as a full time paper designer and teaches her craft on side. You can read her story later.

Christine's story will help you understand what it means to say "yes" to chances, as she has made herself several different income streams.

During a time without many castings but a strong longing for additional purpose in her life, Carola started a fashion blog that has become very popular. All these women have patchwork careers, so their lives never get monotonous. Here's Carola's full interview. ◆

Carola Pojer

ACTRESS & BLOGGER, VIENNA

If someone doesn't give you the dream position you want to have, you have to create the dream position for yourself. Carola is a chance maker. She started her blog, *VIENNA WEDEKIND*, to keep herself occupied when she was running low on acting offers. She knows that as an actress, there might be times when you don't shoot any movies or act on stage, which is why it's important to create projects that work on your own terms. Being an actress, you need the spotlight to be able to entertain the audience; sometimes that means that you have to create the stage yourself, and that's exactly what Carola did.

135

What did you study and why?

I studied photography for a year and then English and psychology for two semesters, which was the time I needed to prepare for auditions at the Academy of Dramatic Arts in Vienna. By the time I was accepted and could start studying drama, I was 21. I finished my formal acting education in 2010.

What happened between your university diploma and your current career?

After finishing my studies, I first wanted to try out different things: theatre, movies, and commercials. I felt I had to see for myself what I really wanted to focus on.

In the beginning, you can't be too picky. You have to build your portfolio and experience what you like doing the most. When applying for theatre positions in German-speaking countries, you must be able to play and sing at least four different characters. So when I was ready for that, I sent out a bunch of applications to all the theatres I was interested in. At the same time, I started applying to acting agencies and went to various movie castings. I hustled!

One of the people I met during that time was a man who more or less mentored me: he enjoyed taking portrait photographs in his spare time and I enjoyed working with him. I suddenly had fresh new images I could use to present myself at the agency. My mentor, this man, was also well-established in the scene and knew the right kind of people, so he introduced me to his circle. Generally speaking, the more people you know and the more people know of you, the easier it will get.

At the beginning, I also worked with a couple of small theatres. It barely paid anything, but it was my way into the scene. I met people who then introduced me to more people and informed me about castings and industry events.

Then, in 2012, I participated in the Berlinale Talent Campus; it was a global casting and the application process was long and very challenging. I happened to be one of the ten people they decided to continue working with. That felt like my first real breakthrough. I was given the opportunity to work with Andie MacDowell, Juliette Binoche, and Keanu Reeves.

After that, I won a casting and got a role in an Austrian TV series. I was invited to the casting and luckily, they were looking for my type. That's when I really felt I had my foot in the industry.

> Generally speaking, the more people you know and the more people know of you, the easier it will get.

How do you find out about castings?

When you start out, it's best to look at the job boards at acting schools. Usually, someone is always on the lookout for actors for their short movies. You need to build a portfolio first before an agent will be interested in working with you.

If you're serious about acting, you can't get your foot in the industry without an agent. They know about different castings and will connect you to the right people. Also, directors mostly approach agents to pre-select the right people for them based on their looks and their character.

How did you make money in the first couple of months?

In the beginning, I didn't make much money. I was working with small theatres and these projects are always on a very tight budget. Nevertheless, you have to go through the experience to meet the right people.

I worked at a department store one day a week and my parents supported me; otherwise, I wouldn't have been able to pay my rent.

From time to time, I got commercial jobs, which are the jobs that pay well compared to all the other jobs you get in the start.

After two years, I had to stop working at the store. It became harder and harder to manage my time and I really wanted to focus on acting full-time.

I had to learn to manage my time and money; sometimes, there are months when you're really busy and earn a lot and then you have months without any jobs or any income.

It's challenging because you have to learn to really save up and keep yourself busy when there are no jobs available to you.

I guess that was why I started blogging: I wanted to make use of my interest in photography and have a continuous project I could focus on when there was nothing else for me to do.

How did you get used to such an unstable situation?

I'm not sure I ever got used to it, but since I started blogging in 2011, I have been fairly busy focusing on my blog, not just on acting. You don't want to be sitting around and staring at your phone, hoping for calls. You have to take charge and find a different activity to occupy your time.

First, I blogged about my experiences as an actress. My blog was a diary of the happenings backstage, but more and more, the blog evolved into a fashion diary, where I've since been capturing my taste and style.

Usually, when there is nothing to do, I try to meet up with as many friends as I can. I know that the time will come when I don't have any time to do anything else but work. I also like to clean out my closet, brainstorm, and look for new ideas. And I read a lot.

137

In the past, there were times when I didn't know what was coming next, which used to be a little daunting, but now I have so much to do with my blog that I don't worry about the future as much as I used to.

Is there something that worries you about your professional future?

I don't know what will happen next year. It's important to find peace with this job because it might happen that an actress doesn't get any acting jobs for one or two years. I try to constantly focus on different creative outlets to keep up my creative spirits. If acting jobs come, then that's great, but I can't rely on it. Especially now, the industry and budgets have been getting smaller, so there are less productions and less money for actors.

How does your blog and your job as an actress correlate? Do you get acting jobs because of your blog?

No, not at all. It's actually the other way around. I get paid to do photography collaborations and trips because I'm an actress. For example, Mulberry and Louis Vuitton both approached me because they liked my energy and it was convenient for them that I wasn't a model, but an actress with a strong profile and character.

Now that I think about it, acting and blogging are very close to each other: when you play in a theatre, you have an immediate response from the audience. You feel the energy and you get a feeling that you've inspired and entertained those watching you. You know what works and what doesn't, which is more or less the same with blogging. When I'm working on a TV series, I don't know how people respond to what I'm doing. It's good to have an outlet where I can be in full control, feel the energy, and get a response immediately. On my blog, it's my script, my design, my thoughts – it's just *me*.

How do you find projects and how do projects find you?

Luckily, they find me. My online presence enables people to know what they will get. I also like to search for photographers and stylists who I would like to work with and then ask them whether they'd like to collaborate.

What did you do to grow the audience of your blog?

That wasn't planned at all. I guess people liked my style and my aesthetics. Instagram helped with catching the attention of people outside Austria who didn't know me from television. Many of my readers came to my blog through Instagram.

What tips would you give to someone who wants to become an actress?

Try to get into the scene to meet as many people as possible. The more people you know, the better your chances are to receive invitations to interesting castings. See if there are any events where the scene gathers and go there. Make friends. Take classes: improv classes are awesome. Get involved in the local scene.

Honestly, just try as many different things as possible until something sticks and then go from there. Don't think too much and learn to be patient and open. You must be able to wait and that might mean that you'll need a side project to keep you busy. Last but not least, don't forget to read. It's important to inform yourself about things that are going on in the world. ●

○ www.carolapojer.com
○ instagram.com/viennawedekind

Turn up your productivity

As Gwen said: "You cannot just write something down on a list, you have to do it too," and when I later asked Olga about her habits to stay productive in her day-to-day, she said productivity doesn't have much to do with using to-do lists; it's about knowing yourself.

I'll let you read her words:

To bridge the gap between 'want' and 'done,' you need to look to your inner self, set up routines, and be very realistic with what your mental self can afford on each given day.

When you fall in love with your to-do list, you fall in love with the number of tasks you cross out. You write down tasks you can easily cross out in a very short amount of time, and later be happy about how much you have accomplished today.

Real productivity is about knowing yourself, being very honest about all the flaws of your own personality, and being very clear on your goals. Productivity is not about to-do lists. It is about listening to yourself and accepting, as well as questioning, the feelings you have.

Why do you do this now?

Why do you go to this event?

Is it important at all?

Why are you so resistant to this particular task?

Ask yourself using 'you' and wait till the answer appears, but don't force the answer and don't rush with a judgement. Give yourself time and space to clarify the targets and the path you should take.

I don't know how about you, but every time I've tried to keep a to-do list, I've always had one or two tasks I kept procrastinating. Then again, I managed to do things which I didn't think were possible, such as writing the first draft of a book in 30 days, and I managed to get these things done without any problems.

Becoming more productive is about having routines, deadlines, and letting people know about what you want to accomplish in order to turn up the social pressure. Once you tell everyone about your big dreams and big goals, you're so much more likely to accomplish them.

141

 While setting yourself a deadline is a great tool to keep yourself in a productive mode, it's also important to say that you're allowed to blow your deadline. Preferences change in life and you should always spend your energy on what's most important to you at a given time. Sometimes, you just can't find any motivation to do anything, and that's all right too because even though you might try to deny it from time to time, you're just a human and humans are never perfect.

One very valuable thing I've learned from reading *No Plot? No Problem!* by Chris Baty was that it's easier to get things done once you already have a lot to do because then it's just one task out of many. It's much harder to get something done when it's the only thing you need to do, which you might recall from the time when you only had to write your final thesis.

But as life is not just fun and games, here are some tools to get the things done where no motivation can ever help:

- ▶ **Post-It notes** – use them for the really uncomfortable tasks; one task, one note, a day is enough
- ▶ **RescueTime** – to block all social media sites and email
- ▶ **The Email Game** – reaching Inbox Zero in a snap
- ▶ **Evernote** – the most synchronized to-do list and keep all your notes in one place
- ▶ **Pocket** – get your reading done later

142

Read on to hear Luna's interview. Speaking of to-do lists, I don't know of anyone else who manages to accomplish as much as she does. ◆

143

Luna Vega

E-COMMERCE CONSULTANT, LOCATION-INDEPENDENT

If there is one word that describes Luna, it's "driven." She knows what she wants and doesn't mind getting up early and going to bed late to make her plans a reality. She consults small fashion businesses and recently published her first book. She is currently on an extended research trip to learn more about digital trends in Asia and how small businesses in Europe and the Americas can profit from connecting to the Asian market. She shares what it takes to build a business and how important consistency is when you want to build a brand online.

145 —

What did you study and why?
Originally, I wanted to become a TV reporter and get into journalism, but I am not a fantastic writer, so I studied political science with a minor in broadcasting. During undergrad, I started working for a radio station in Miami. Being there made me realize how much I loved communication.

What happened between your university diploma and your current career?
Straight out of university, I started working in the technology industry. In 2001, I moved to Paris where I worked for a special effects company. I was a producer and worked with so many amazing people. I had my dream job!

As you can imagine, the internet wasn't what it is nowadays. We sent a couple of emails, but every time we tried to upload a video, it took forever.

After two and a half years in France, I was curious to know what else the world had to offer me, so I returned to the US. I found a program that specialized in telecommunication at NYU (Interactive Telecommunications Program) and I applied for it. I'd say that being accepted was like my digital birth because since my graduation at NYU, I've been working for digital advertising agencies or on digital projects.

So, what made you decide to go freelance and start consulting small fashion businesses online?

I think I was a bit traumatized after working in advertising agencies: it's normal to work 60 hours plus a week and I had a hard time keeping myself motivated. I felt as though there was something else out there that could better suit my personality.

In 2006, I built my own website and started experimenting with consulting. Years later in 2010, I took the plunge and became a freelance consultant. It was mostly because an agency asked me whether I was interested in working with them on a freelance contract. I've been self-employed since.

I've spent a lot of years networking, so once people knew I was available, the phone kept ringing and I never had to worry about finding the next assignment.

I usually work on assignments at a digital agency for a couple of months and then I focus on consulting small fashion businesses until I feel I should earn more money to make sure I can return to building up the business I am most truly passionate about.

As an entrepreneur, you have to have faith in yourself. Success doesn't come overnight. It's a slow and a painful process. It takes time to establish yourself.

How did you make money in the first couple of months?

When I first started, I didn't quit my job. I lived in New York for many years, and there you can't sustain yourself if you're not making enough income. I worked as a digital producer for an agency Monday through Friday from nine until five, but I also did some consultancy on the side. When I saved up enough money and the projects were over, I focused full-time on building my own consultancy for small businesses and because I had enough money, I could grow my business organically.

I've learned to be extremely organized and disciplined to reach my aims. Often, I would wake up as early as 6 AM, go to a Starbucks to focus on my book, leave to go to work, and then I continued working on my book and relaunching my business when I got home in the evening.

In 2014, I stayed with an agency for an entire year. I knew I wanted to go on a research trip to Asia to better understand what's going on in the digital scene there and I had to save up to be able to focus on writing my second book. As an entrepreneur, you have to have faith in yourself. Success doesn't come overnight. It's a slow and a very painful process. It takes time to establish yourself online.

How do you find clients and how do they find you?

I consider myself lucky because my clients usually find me. It's mostly through word-of-mouth because former clients recommend me to my new clients.

If you don't have connections, then don't be afraid to reach out to people on LinkedIn. Send a personal message to people you're interested in meeting. Do some research and really be personal and relevant. If they're in the same city, try to meet up for a coffee. Be proactive. I believe that being proactive and sincere will set you apart from the majority.

What do you do in times when you don't have any projects?

I usually work on my own brand. I always try to find time to think about how to add value to people's businesses. I'm trying to develop my own voice that's understandable to people who don't know much about marketing.

How much do you plan ahead?

I don't really plan ahead to be honest. I know my goals, but I don't necessarily set myself fixed deadlines, mainly to avoid disappointing or discouraging myself. Every time I had set myself a deadline in the past, I blew it.

For example, when I was working on the book, I wanted to publish it in January, but only managed to publish it in April. I didn't think of all the other things that were required after you've completed writing the content. You have to design the interior of the book, design a cover, and complete all of the little things you don't think about when you start.

I saw publishing the book as a way for me to relaunch my business. I planned to only start the Podcast, the Global Influencer, and my Youtube channel after the book was published. I regret not having started earlier because I could have gathered my audience already during the process.

So while I don't necessarily plan ahead, I do have a set of goals I want to accomplish. Over the years, I've learned how important consistency is. In the beginning, I only published content irregularly, but you can only build an audience if you make what you do a habit and publish something consistently.

148

In the future, I want to plan six months ahead and try to stay focused. Sometimes, I worry if I'm wasting my time and if I should instead just lie in the sun and drink margaritas, but then I remind myself of my goals and keep hustling. It clearly takes time.

> I've learned to publish content even when I wasn't 100% satisfied. There's always room to practice and improve.

How do you structure your days?
It depends if I work on a project at an agency or if I only focus on my own clients. When I'm at the agency, I work nine to five and then do everything else before and after work.

If I don't have an agency contract, then I wake up early, work from 7 AM until 10 or 11, go for a run, have lunch, take the afternoon off, and then get back to work around 4 PM and focus until 9 or 10 in the evening.

How do you represent yourself online? What platforms do you consider important?
I have my own blog and my website: I use Wordpress.

I'm on Facebook, but I don't give it much longer, maybe another year. The interest and success rates for Facebook business pages have been decreasing, so it's just not practical to me anymore.

I do use Twitter and Instagram, and because the popularity of video content has been on the rise, I'm experimenting a lot with Youtube these days. In the beginning, I tried to make everything perfect, but at that point, you're only making things harder for yourself. I've learned to publish content even when I wasn't 100% satisfied. There's always room to practice and improve.

What would you recommend to someone who wants to become a freelance consultant?

I'm not a believer of doing it with just 50 cents in your pocket. I think that you need a job to keep yourself afloat and take time on the side to figure it out; get a feel for the market.

The best way to start is to go to meetups and networking events. I've always been trying to connect to as many people as possible because I believe that knowing the right people is the best way to attract new clients. At the end of the day, it's about who you know.

Also, start by creating a website for yourself. Think about how you want to work with people and let people know how they can work with you. Consider if you want to charge an hourly rate or a standard-fee for a certain service. What also works best is doing research on LinkedIn to look if people need someone with your special skillset. In the worst case, try out oDesk or Elance. ●

○ www.lunavega.net
○ twitter.com/misslunavega

Earn (more) money

The major trap of freelancing is that your business is fully dependent on you and your personal well-being. Once you're sick or on holidays, you have no income, which is why so many freelancers end up not taking time off from work.

The only way to solve this is by working even more; at least temporarily! You need to build a passive income stream that will make you money while you're busy doing other things. In other words, you need to find a way to package yourself up. If you are a service provider, just as the majority of freelancers are, then find a way to create a product based on your knowledge and skills.

Akilah earns money with the videos she made and published on Youtube, Frankie makes about 5–10 % of her income with her books, and Diana gets royalties from her fonts.

The money doesn't have to be much, but it will make you feel better when you have at least some money coming in while you're on holidays.

Probably the hardest part is finding a way that works for you and your business. Youtube has become a great service that can make you some money on side. Many people search for tutorials on Youtube, so if you can teach something, Youtube might be the right answer for you. If you're a graphic designer, try to find services, such as GraphicRiver or Threadless, to sell your designs. Even designing themes for Wordpress might be a way to generate passive income. As a photographer, try to get your pictures up on EyeEm or iStockphoto. To give you a personal example, I have about 100 images up on Getty Images and so far, I've made about $45 in four months, which isn't much, but given that I never intended to make any money with my photography, it's pretty good.

Building additional income streams will help you make sure that if a client ever stops working with you, it won't matter as much because you won't be dependent on a single source of income. Building a passive income stream might be one way of how you work "on" your business and also a way to boost your savings account. If you decide for yourself that building a passive income stream is a good idea, set time aside to do it and make it part of your routine, and also, don't forget to set deadlines.

151 —

One of the most talented people I know who runs a portfolio business with various passive income streams is Christine, a well-known German blogger, author, and video producer. Read her interview on the following pages. ◆

Christine Neder

DIGITAL CONTENT PRODUCER, BERLIN

Interesting people don't just have stories; they create stories and are really good at telling them. Christine is known because of her blog, her two books that were published by Schwarzkopf & Schwarzkopf, and her appearances on television. Here, she sheds some light on building a portfolio and how to make oneself more appealing to potential clients.

What did you study and why?

Originally, I studied fashion design in Bielefeld. I wanted to do something creative, and it was easy for me to relate to sewing because my grandmother was a tailor. During my studies, I realized that I wasn't that great at making clothes, so I thought I could work as a stylist instead. One of my internships was with the German *Vogue* and while I worked there, I always felt a bit envious of the people who wrote all the editorials. Another internship I did was in New York, which felt like a great reason to start a blog to keep friends and family up-to-date on my daily adventures.

What happened between your university diploma and your current career?

I moved to Munich and took on another internship; this time with the German edition of *Elle Magazine*. I liked Munich a lot and wanted to stay, but I wasn't lucky with getting any more work after my internship at Elle was over. That's why I started applying for work in Berlin.

When I had to move, I wasn't really feeling like moving in a flatshare again and because I didn't know anyone, I didn't want to live on my own either. I came up with the idea for *90 Nights, 90 Beds,* which started as a blog project and eventually turned into a book. The idea for *90 Nights, 90 Beds* was to couchsurf in Berlin for three months and stay with different people every night and then write about it.

I first learned about *couchsurfing* on a trip to Romania and really liked the concept. My blog was starting to become a little boring and I needed something fresh. It seemed like fun to sleep somewhere different every night, see all these different flats, and meet different people in their private homes.

The project got a great response from the media, and one day I had an email from a publisher in my mailbox asking me if I'd like to write a book about what I had experienced.

Once you've written a book, it's much easier to get jobs and write for newspapers and magazines. It's not that I would have made a lot of money with the book, but it has been a great reference for my work.

After I finished my internship, someone asked me to become their social media manager because they noticed I was good at entertaining an online community. Then, I worked for a German newspaper before I had a concept for my second book that allowed me to visit 40 festivals in 40 weeks. From then on, I focused on my blog and work related to it. I was mostly producing content for various media.

You started to blog fairly early; how has the content of your blog evolved?

My texts have always been very personal. I started blogging in 2007 when I was in New York. I wanted to write about my experiences and a little bit about fashion because I was there to attend the New York Fashion Week.

After I graduated, I went on a vacation to Thailand and just continued writing about the daily happenings. I enjoyed writing about my travels and experiences. As far as I'm concerned, the content of my blog has always been a mixture of travel, lifestyle, and personal texts.

What were your first steps to become a digital content producer and blogger?

I never planned for my blog to become a business. I wanted to travel and it sounded appealing to travel for free. I just had to figure out how to make money from it.

I quickly figured out that the only way for me to make money while traveling was by adding value to people's businesses. I taught myself how to make videos and because I can come up with a storyline and then shoot and cut the videos; my services are much more affordable than what a professional team would charge.

I also take fairly good pictures. So, it's not that I would only live off my blog, but my blog definitely is my extended business card. When people see something I've done and published online and they like it enough to have similar content on their own social media channels, that's when they contact me.

When I decided to become more serious about my blog, I created a media kit where I summarized what I can do for my clients and how they can work with me.

155

How were you making money in the beginning?

I didn't start my blog to make money with it, but it did serve me well as a digital portfolio for what I do. When I attended the 40 festivals – when I spent 40 weeks traveling – that wasn't necessarily paying me much, but it was a good way for me to build a portfolio.

There are several ways how I make money: one is through my blog with advertorials and cooperations. I also produce content for other people's social media channels, I consult people and help them with their social strategy, and sometimes, I even run other brands' social media channels.

> Attending the 40 festivals and spending 40 weeks traveling wasn't necessarily paying me much, but it was a good way for me to build a portfolio.

On side, I also have a video production company together with my partner. I work on the editorials and he shoots and cuts the content we produce.

What's your favorite type of collaborations?

I like when companies send me somewhere and then I can explore the area, write blog posts for my blogs, and shoot some videos. When they go on to buy my photos and videos, then that's just perfect! I think that because I offer my clients a full service, it works to my advantage. Of course, they could send a professional photographer and maybe get better pictures than the ones I take, but with me, they have someone who can take decent pictures, make videos, and write about it.

I consider myself lucky because I don't have to look for clients anymore. They come to me through my website. I'm at the point where I can choose who I want to work with. There are so many bloggers who only post advertorials, and I think it's sad. When I first started, none of us were thinking about making money from blogging; it was considered a passionate side project.

When I choose who I want to work with, I always look for collaborations that fit with the concept of my blog and with my own personality. It must add value to the lives of my readers because without them, none of this would ever be possible.

I quickly figured out that the only way for me to make money while traveling was by adding value to people's businesses.

How did you teach yourself to do all these different things?

I learned some of the basics at uni, but most of the time, I looked up online tutorials on Youtube or asked people I worked with to teach me some of their skills. When I first started producing video content, I was editing everything in iMovie. Then I taught myself how to use Final Cut.

How do you organize your days?

My days are rarely the same. Some days I write, then there are times that I'm traveling and don't have much time to do any administration or anything else really. When I get back to Berlin, the city I'm based in, I try to work through my emails and reply back to everyone.

I'm always on the lookout for new ideas. Also, I'm currently writing a novel and looking for a new publishing house than the one

I published the previous books with. I always try to plan a month ahead and sometimes, I even know what I'll be doing in two months.

How do you represent yourself online and what platforms do you use?

I have my blog, a Youtube channel, and a Facebook, Twitter, Instagram, and Pinterest account. I'm also working on my website where I detail what people can hire me for because most people know me as a blogger, but I do so much more!

Could you give some practical tips to someone who wants to become a professional blogger?

157 ——

Be patient: it takes a really long time to build it up. Be as real and genuine as possible. Always be the best *you* you can be to strive for what you want and don't give up. ●

○ www.lilies-diary.com
○ instagram.com/lilies_diary

Teach your skills

Although the "maker movement" has been going strong for a while, it's still hard to compete with high-street retailers that have their stock produced in countries with cheap labor. Of course, there are many reasons why your products cost more than products bought at a mainstream store, being you probably produce locally and have to pay people accordingly.

One of the main insights I've gained during my research for this book is that teaching is a popular way to earn some fixed income. We live in the so-called "knowledge society," and the amount of stuff people own has been on a decrease for a while already. In my opinion, what has been on the rise is our hunger for knowledge and our interest in gaining additional skills to be able to make things ourselves.

If you're a product-driven business or are trying to setup a business that sells goods, and are looking for ways to add additional income streams, try to think of what you could teach people. For example, you could teach the steps of your production process or the knowledge that you've gained over the years.

If you're worried that sharing knowledge will ruin your business, I assure you that instead, it will help you gain the reputation of an expert and create a community. People might want to learn skills, but they might not necessarily want to start a business based on what they've learned from you; if they do, they'll reference you as their greatest source of inspiration and knowledge for the rest of their lives. What a privilege!

There are several ways to make teaching an additional source of income: if you get a possibility and are feeling comfortable with standing in the classroom, you might want to look into teaching opportunities at a local college, just like Aisha does. You can also run workshops yourself, just like Diana or Lisa: Diana started a meetup group where she teaches calligraphy to people who want to do something creative in the evening after their nine-to-five jobs. Lisa announces her origami workshops on Instagram and usually has about twelve people on average join her classes where she gives lessons on folding paper.

Anyone who is even a little outgoing can give classes to small groups: if you are, for instance, a fashion designer, you can teach people how to create beautiful fashion visualizations or how to choose the right fabrics for a collection. If you are a skilled consultant, you could give lectures to beginners and share some of your personal insights.

You might think that what you know is general knowledge, but that's not always the case because it's very unlikely that people are dealing with the same insights as you in their day-to-day. Teaching can even give you a new perspective on what you do and provide you with additional ideas.

You can also tape yourself and upload videos to Youtube, or write blog posts and share your knowledge online. This, of course, won't necessarily generate an income for you, but there's a good chance it will increase the visibility of your brand. Read about Aisha, who teaches at the university where she once studied and see what it has done for her. ◆

Aisha Franz

COMIC ARTIST & ILLUSTRATOR, BERLIN

When she was a little girl, she drew comics, and that's exactly what Aisha has been doing ever since. She has had two graphic novels published and has been working as an illustrator for various clients and publications. The interview with Aisha helps clarify how to make clients find you and your work, as well as how you can best serve them once you're hired.

What did you study and why?
I studied communication design with a focus on comics in Kassel, Germany. My initial goal was to become an animator, but it always frustrated me how long it took to actually animate. It's a very time-consuming procedure. Comics and illustrations just felt right on the other hand. They were much quicker to make.

What happened between your university diploma and your current career?
I represented our university at the Comic Salon in Erlangen. It's the biggest comic fair in Germany and they have a special area just for universities. I wasn't finished with my graduation project back then, but I brought all my drawings with me because I thought I had nothing to lose. I showed them to everyone who was interested and that's also how my publisher found me.

Without even realizing it, I was suddenly a published comic artist. They offered to publish the graphic novel I created for my graduation. Since then, I've done readings and workshops and also started doing illustration work for various clients.

The publishing house works like an agent, so now whenever people have a project, they first talk to my publisher who then contacts me. The comic world is very small, so it's important to get to know the right people who work within the industry.

What made you decide to become a freelance illustrator?
I can't really say I decided to become one consciously. It all had its own dynamic. I felt I found my calling, and I couldn't really imagine

doing anything else but drawing. The only challenge was to figure out how to make money doing it because comics are more an underground arts style. Comics artists mostly earn money by doing illustration work. I just had to find a balance between my comics work, my real passion, and the work I do for clients.

How did you make money in the first couple of months?

Although I was teaching at workshops, illustrating, and holding readings, up until very recently, I was working in a café. I worked there for about two years after my graduation, until one day I realized that I didn't need that source of income anymore.

162

My boss at the café was flexible and very supportive, so I was able to work less and less over time. When you work on illustrations, you must be fast and flexible because the deadlines are always very tight.

After university, I also applied for a couple of artist residencies, such as with the Goethe Institute, and that gave me space, time, and money to be able to focus on creating art. At the beginning, you have to look for grants to be able to focus on building a portfolio.

> Be productive and work on your own style. There is nothing embarrassing about being authentic.

I'm still trying to find a balance and don't have it all planned out. Sometimes, I don't know what will happen in the next month, but so far, it's all been working out just fine!

What were your first steps to become a freelance illustrator?

I was basically self-employed already during my studies. I regularly had small projects on site, so it was helpful to get a feel for how it is to be self-employed while I wasn't dependent on the income. Invoicing and finding the right price for your work takes time. It still feels like a battle because I have to be a business person and not just an artist.

I personally find the business side of being a freelancer a real challenge. You have to deal with invoicing; setting your own price. It's always a relief for me when people tell me in advance how much they can pay and then I either agree and take the job or not.

I think it's really difficult to set my own price because when I am excited about a project, I want to do it regardless of what the budget is, but then I remind myself that this money has to also pay my rent and all my other expenses. I don't do what I do for the money, so this really bothers me sometimes.

Recently, I started teaching, so I will have a more steady income in the future. At the same time, I will have to be more organized when it comes to budgeting my time. It's important to me to spend at least a third of my time on personal projects to be able to evolve my art and my style.

163

What do you struggle with the most in your profession?
I think the hardest part is figuring out a daily rhythm; putting time aside to work on your own projects and really developing your style. You also have to sign on to do things you actually *want* to be doing, regardless of whether they pay you at this moment or not.

How do you find clients and how do they find you?
Many clients find me through my Tumblr. The moment I started my Tumblr, I really noticed that projects started coming in. I also use Facebook to showcase my work.

Additionally, I have a collective of fellow illustrators here in Berlin. When someone talks to one of us and the client doesn't like this illustrator's style, then the illustrator always refers the person to someone else in the group.

This also works online. If one of us is featured on a blog or in a magazine, the person who writes the piece often finds the whole collective and then mentions all of us, which has been very beneficial to every single illustrator in the group.

How do you feel when someone takes your work and uses it on their blog?
I think it's flattering. Most of the time, people tell me before they

publish the article. Sometimes they send me a quick note afterwards to inform me that they did. Everything I publish online is under Creative Commons, so I'm happy for people to use my work as long as they also state my name.

How do you keep your clients happy?
I always try to be myself and be very honest. For example, I always send several sketches and ask what the client thinks. I involve them in the process and build a relationship, and they appreciate that. Clients also respect the fact that I respond quickly to their inquiries.

164

Could you give some practical tips to someone who wants to become a freelance illustrator?
First of all, having a website is mandatory. If you have good work, it has to be available online and easily accessible. Even if you don't have any clients, you have to be your own client and constantly produce new work and share it online. Be productive and work on your own style.

It's important to see yourself as a creator; an author with a certain edge. Don't try to apply a formula you think is right. Take time, develop your own style, practice it, and utilize it.

Then there is networking. It's crucial to get to know fellow illustrators and the creative community. If you want to draw comics, go to fairs and talk to people. Be present. ●

○ www.fraufranz.com
○ aishafranz.tumblr.com

Set your price

One of the hardest parts for someone who's about to start free-lancing is setting a price, advocating it in front of the client, and negotiating if the client doesn't want to pay the requested rate.

Before you start thinking about your hourly rate, ask yourself how much you need a month, then add the costs of your health insurance and taxes. This amount is different in every country.

Once you have the amount you need to earn per month, think about how much you'd like to earn per month. Now, think about how many hours you want and need to work to be able to achieve the amount of money you're aiming for. Also, ascertain the lowest, equivalent hourly rate you're willing to work for. Got it? Great!

All these numbers are probably very different, so how should you set the price to start with?

Are you going to be able to get as many clients as you'll need to reach the amount of money you want? Or can you tolerate a little less pay because you have an opportunity to work on a project of a lifetime, which you're dying to have in your portfolio? Do you already have enough references of your previous work experience that will help you justify the amount you want, or do you need to ask for the amount you need, to first build a portfolio?

Another decision you'll have to make is how you want to charge your clients: do you want to charge per hour, per day, per week, a flat-rate, or, as it is common in some branches such as copywriting or translating, per word?

Generally speaking, many freelancers who have been in business for a while are turning away from charging per hour because it automatically caps your maximum earning potential. If you charge on a job basis, your only limit is your speed in which you are able to accomplish the job. This will help you work more productively and thus, your hourly rate might even triple in the long run.

Last but not least, how much are people in your industry and your area charging for the same kind of services? Do you know someone you could ask? Or will you have to do a little research to get an idea for how much you can ask? You can always humbly approach someone you admire and ask them to help you decide. People are really supportive, so don't hesitate to ask!

Sometimes, you'll have people approach you because they like what they found about you online and they'll openly tell you how much their budget is. In those cases, it's your decision if you have enough resources to take on the job and if the project is what you want to have in your portfolio to be able to attract similar projects in the future.

Once you set your price, advocate it! You need to make a living just like everyone else. It seems that the common perception is that clients are after a cheap deal, but I believe that we've all come to understand that the cheapest deal, in most cases, doesn't lead to a qualitative outcome. While you can compete with competitors based on their rates, you most certainly shouldn't.

There are many people out there who make their living off platforms such as Elance, PeoplePerHour, or 99designs, and while it might work for some, and it might even work for you to test the waters of freelancing, I'd recommend that you find a specialized niche in order to charge higher rates. *Stop Thinking Like a Freelancer* by Liam Veitch might give you some additional tricks on how to distinguish yourself from the masses to be able to increase your pay rates. Let's go back to negotiating for a minute. Whenever your client isn't willing to pay you what you asked for, don't just lower the price and settle. Instead, decrease the amount of services you'll deliver. What I usually do is I allow the client two feedback loops and add some other additional services that don't necessarily cost me more time. If the client isn't able or willing to pay the rate I initially suggested, I decrease the amount of services and only then will I lower the price.

Your price is your value per hour, so you shouldn't end up working and later think how underpaid the job is. Everything you do should always add value to your business, either financially or as a reference.

168

Here are some additional thoughts on negotiating prices with clients from Rafaela. ◆

Rafaela Mota Lemos

TRANSLATOR, LOCATION-INDEPENDENT

"The only thing you need to change your life is the right attitude; and the right attitude is to be curious." Rafa always thinks at least one step ahead. Finding herself questioning if being a successful freelancer was the peek of her career, she had to find something new to challenge herself. She decided to pack her bags and move countries every couple of months to experience how it is to live in Rio, New York, and Tel Aviv. She shares her strategies to stay focused in her interview, and how she tackles the intimidating task of charging and negotiating rates with her clients; something she isn't comfortable doing at all.

171

What did you study and why?
I thought I had a talent for languages, which is why I studied translation and interpreting. I consider myself very lucky to be working in that field because only about ten out of the 500 students became translators.

What happened between your university diploma and your current career?
In my last year of university, I was done with all my classes, so I took the chance to participate in the Erasmus program and moved to Milan. That's where I learned Italian, which has proven extremely beneficial. There are not many people in Portugal who can translate Italian to Portuguese; I created a niche for myself.

I was able to take whatever classes I was interested in; I studied history, cinema, Italian, and French literature. I partied almost every night and really enjoyed myself there.

After my Erasmus semester, I decided to stay in Milan. I lived there for three years and worked in online marketing, but always kept translating on side.

In 2009, I moved back to Portugal and started working for a translation agency as a project manager. It was important to me to gain that experience because my initial plan has always been to open my own agency, so I wanted to have different perspectives on the business.

In 2012, I decided to quit my job and only work freelance. I now work for various translation agencies, mostly with Italian clients.

What made you decide to become a freelance translator and what made you decide to become location-independent?
I was young when I had my first full-time job. I'm someone who always thinks about the next step. When I started my first job, I was 22, and after three days I caught myself wondering what my next job would be.

So, when I eventually became a freelancer, I thought to myself, 'Am I really going to be a service provider for the rest of my life? Is this it?!'

Earning more money couldn't really be my motivation, so I needed something else to work towards. I kept stumbling upon articles about people who traveled and worked remotely. That rung a bell!

I'm not a backpacker kind of girl, but I did want to have the experience of living in other countries, so in 2013, I picked five cities where I wanted to live for an extended period of time and booked my flights. I chose Rio, New York, Tel Aviv, Naples, and Luanda. I usually plan for my accommodation and look for coworking spaces about two months in advance.

When you first started working as a freelancer, how did it go in the beginning?
I wasn't happy with my job, so I quit on a wild card. I had to give two months notice, so I basically knew that I had two months to figure things out.

I've always been freelancing on the side, so I already had some clients but I didn't have any savings. Everyone always says that you should have about six months worth of salary. I didn't because when I work, I like to travel, have dinner with friends, go out, and party. I don't count my pennies!

I had to straighten out my finances, so I started counting and organizing myself. First, I realized that I was making two times more in the evenings than what I was earning in my full-time job. I had to laugh: why did I waste my time in a job I didn't enjoy for so long?

Then, I counted all the open invoices I had and there were in total something like € 6,000 for which I never issued any invoices. It was all very small sums, but collectively in total, it was actually a really big chunk of money! It wasn't planned, and for the first time I felt kind of lucky for being so disorganized with my accountancy.

Seeing what I saw, I had to acknowledge that we women are very good at sabotaging ourselves. I wasn't sure if I could pull it off for so long, but then, once I sat down and looked at where I was at, I knew I'd be fine.

I was afraid of Murphy's law; that I would quit my job and my clients would drop me. To my surprise, however, once I announced I was going to freelance full-time, more and more work started coming in.

173

How much time do you plan ahead with your professional projects?

My work flow is unpredictable. I'm literally always busy; sometimes more, sometimes less. I do have to admit that I'm not the greatest time manager in the world, so I'm probably wasting a lot of time

So, when I eventually became a freelancer, I thought to myself, 'Am I really going to be a service provider for the rest of my life? Is this it?!'

with unnecessary tasks or activities. After almost three years, I still work almost seven days a week to meet the deadlines, but that's mostly because I struggle staying focused.

How do you charge your clients?

With most clients, I charge per word and then there are some clients who pay per hour. In general, I can easily make € 2,000 a month. In a good month, the ones in which I don't get to sleep, I can make € 5,000. I once read that when you work too much, you have to raise your rates. After I read it, I realized I was working way too much, so I decided to choose five of my clients and I asked them if they would still give me work if I raised my rates. I wasn't confident enough to just tell them, 'I'm raising my rates.' I was very careful with how I phrased my question. They negotiated me down, but it was the beginning of me learning how to speak up.

How do you find clients and how do they find you?

I'm part of various networks for translators such as Proz.com. Tumblr, for example, approached me on Proz. I know they interviewed several linguists and I got the contract with them.

You know how people often say that you need a linear career to succeed? Or they'll say that freelancing is the ultimate goal and that it's not so important what you had done before? I don't believe any of this is true because every experience you have shapes you in a certain way. I am proud of my previous experiences because they helped me get the really interesting jobs. For instance, I know I got Tumblr as my client because I worked in online marketing and social media when I started my career in Italy, after Erasmus, which made me stand out. I worked with them from 2012 to the beginning of 2015.

How do you organize your work days?

My deadlines are always very tight, so things can get pretty busy. I also struggle with procrastination. I often end up working for 10 hours, not because I would actually work for 10 hours, but because I tend to get distracted with other things in the middle (writing, blogging, social media, catching up with friends all around the world, etc).

I've been using the Pomodoro technique for a few years now, which is a system that breaks your work into 'pomodoros,' which are 25-minute-long work sessions and after every pomodoro, you can take a five minute break. It sounds like a short period of time, but you can actually get a lot of work done. After four pomodoros, you can have a 30 minute break, where you can do whatever you want to do: check Facebook, emails, or Skype with your friends.

I've been doing much better since I got my alarm clock and started tracking my time like this.

How do you represent yourself online? What platforms do you use?
I truly am an early adopter because every time a new network launches, I'm the first one to check it out. I use Facebook, Twitter, Instagram, and I have my blog, which I've been publishing articles on since 2006.

Could you give some practical tips to someone who wants to become a location independent translator?
After all of these years, I do think that you should have a buffer of 175
at least € 3,000 at all times. Even if it's just for your peace of mind, I think peace of mind is the most important thing money can buy.

Before you hit the road, you should have a solid business and regular calls from clients who don't mind where you are. Of course, you can go to cheaper places, but if you plan to live in cities such as Rio or New York, knowing where the money's coming from is essential.

What I've learned is that you can only live in one place at a time. Don't waste your time missing home. You will miss out on a lot of events in people's lives who are important to you and that is something you must learn to accept. Focus on where you are and try to make the most out of it. That's the advice I would give to everyone who's already out of the door with one foot.

To everyone who thinks they don't have enough money or they have another excuse that's holding them back, I'd say that as long as you don't have any children or parents you're responsible for, you're free to go. If you don't pay rent in your hometown, you can pay rent anywhere else in the world. You might not be able to go and live in Tokyo, but you might have enough money to live in Spain or Italy.

Your life doesn't have to be perfect and you definitely don't have to be rich to travel. The only thing you need is the right attitude and the right attitude is to be curious.

I'm not rich. Sometimes, at the end of the month, I have € 80 in my bank account, but I have learned something: money always comes! If your wish is to be a freelancer, then try it out. If it doesn't work, then you can always look for another job and that's okay. You'll never know unless you try. Be curious. That's all! ●

○ www.odisseando.com
○ twitter.com/rafaelalemos

177

Treat your customers well

It costs about five times as much to acquire a new customer than to keep one; not just money, but energy. So, how do you engage customers and make them come back for more, and how do you make sure your customers talk about you?

Social media is an instant click away, and it's much more likely that your followers have a higher following than you could ever build yourself. You should engage your customers and give them something they'll take a picture of: for product based businesses, packaging is the ultimate answer. A nicely wrapped product or a note you include in your package can make all the difference.

Once you've finalized your order and delivered it to a happy customer, include people in your mailing list and reach out to them regularly. You don't have to send out weekly newsletters, but make sure you reach out to people who have bought your product in the past and update them on the latest offers at least every couple of months.

If you're a service provider and can't send nicely wrapped packages to your customers, make sure your work experience with others is mutually positive and don't hesitate to ask for a recommendation once you've delivered.

Make it your business to reach out to former clients to ask them how their business is going and wish them all the best on special occasions, such as Christmas or New Years. Make sure your former customers see that you didn't just want to make money, but that you genuinely care about their success. Send a card, a present, or some promotional merchandise and keep your former customers close, even if you're not working for them at that particular moment.

If someone's dissatisfied with your services, see it as a chance to surprise them by your willingness to cooperate and solve their issue. If you manage to solve someone's problem, they'll be pleasantly surprised and much more dedicated to help you make your business successful; they might then even refer you to their friends to utilize your excellent service. Sometimes, that means that you'll have to give them their money back, and that's also something you should calculate when you set your price.

179

At the end, you should always make sure everyone thinks positively about you. No matter the disagreement, you should never make the other person feel like an idiot or inferior. If a mistake occurs, treat it objectively and make it your mistake; show your human weakness or blame the universe; NEVER the other person. If there is a problem, only use the word "I" and never use the word "you" because instantly, people will defend themselves, and acting defensively never helped solve any issue.

But let's look at the flip side: over-delivery. Surprise your customers and treat them the way you'd like to be treated yourself. Here's Lisa's story. ◆

Lisa Marie Andersson

PAPER DESIGNER, GÖTHENBURG

Up The Wooden Hills is Lisa's brand and brainchild. Not only does she have an online store, she also produces paper art on behalf of various brand and design agencies and she runs workshops where she teaches people how to create their own origami art. Here, Lisa explains how she built a business people love and share with their friends, as well as the importance of being personal, transparent, and most of all, thankful.

What did you study and why?
First, I studied art history and visual studies at a university in Göthen-
burg. Afterwards, I studied project management where I specialized in management within the cultural sector.

What happened between your university diploma and your current career?
I worked in the fashion industry; first at Très Bien, a menswear fashion store in Malmö. Then I moved to Göthenburg where I worked as a PR manager for Permanent Vacation, a women's fashion brand, which was my last job before I founded *Up The Wooden Hills*.

What made you decide to start your own business?
I think I was just tired of working for other people and I wanted to do my own thing instead. I started making dresses and selling them online. Not everyone could afford to buy my clothes, so I was looking for a complimentary product line I could offer at a lower price. I wanted to create something small and affordable.

I've always been crafting and one day I printed a pattern and folded it. I thought it looked quite good and put it up in my online store. I created a collection of origami sculptures and posted some pictures on my Instagram and it somehow went from there. People started ordering my paper sculptures and at some point, I was getting so many orders for my paper craft that it made more sense to just focus on that. The transition felt very natural.

How did you make money in the first couple of months?

When I first started with my fashion brand back in 2010, I applied for governmental support. If the country where you live offers funding to small businesses, then you should inform yourself and apply.

I wrote a business plan and received money that paid for my living expenses for the first six months. I was able to focus on building a brand full-time, which felt like a real luxury at that time. Luckily, I was already making some money in the beginning, but it definitely wasn't enough for me to live off of.

My parents were very supportive and gave me some money too. It was tough and it took years for me to become stable and live off my handcraft. I only started earning enough in the spring of 2013. I didn't manage to make a living out of my fashion business, but it works now that I'm a paper designer.

How do you make a living as a paper designer?

I earn a small part of my income with the paper sculptures, which I sell in my online shop and through various interior shops in France and Sweden. I also run workshops to teach people how to fold origami. I really enjoy getting immediate feedback and sharing the joy of helping people create something beautiful. I also work for different agencies, which makes for the majority of my income and enables me to focus on the other parts of my business.

I follow up on every order and send my customers a personal note and a confirmation email. I make sure I inform my customers as soon as their order is on the way, too.

What did you do to grow your business?

Just like everyone who runs a business, I worked incredibly hard. In my last job, when I worked in PR at the Très Bien shop, I learned a lot about social media and how to use it in a professional context. I had my own blog, and I used Facebook and Instagram.

Now, I don't post on my personal blog anymore and only focus on Instagram where I publish pictures of my work about once a day. Over the years, my audience grew to about 50,000 followers.

Most of my customers find my shop through Instagram, Pinterest, or when other people blog about my workshops and paper creations.

How do you make sure your customers buy from you repeatedly or refer you to their friends?

I have a very personal approach and believe in transparency, so I always try to provide as much information as possible. I follow up on every order and send my customers a personal note and a confirmation email. I make sure I inform my customers as soon as their order is on the way too.

I think it's important to be thankful. I always try to answer every comment on my social media channels. I really hope that is what makes people believe in my business and order repeatedly or refer my workshops to their friends.

How do you announce your classes?

Usually on Instagram, on Facebook, and on my website. Also, when I meet people, I tell them that I run crafting classes where I teach how to fold paper. I usually welcome ten to twelve people to my workshops. I want to make sure everyone's having a good time and no one feels left behind.

How long do you plan ahead?

Not too far ahead to be honest. My next goal is to learn how to build a sustainable business and plan ahead. I've signed up for a program that will teach me what I have to do to be able to foresee how my business will be doing and eventually, what I'll be doing in six months or maybe even a year.

183

Could you give some practical tips to someone who wants to become a professional designer?

What I've learned is that you don't necessarily need a formal education in design to become a designer. If you're passionate about something and dedicated to making it work, you can and you should try!

Just really take some time to think things through: think about what you want your brand to look like and how you want people to feel about your brand. Think about the ways you want to advertise your business. Also, consider what additional products you could offer to expand your business. If I didn't make and try to sell my origami sculptures in my fashion store, I wouldn't be where I am today.

Because you can't know everything, you should surround yourself with great people and don't be afraid to ask for advice or assistance. If your country has a funding program for young entrepreneurs, then don't hesitate and apply! ●

○ www.upthewoodenhills.com
○ instagram.com/upthewoodenhills

Lisa Marie Andersson • Paper Designer, Göthenburg

Scale your business

As a freelancer, you're most likely a one-woman business, at least in the beginning. Unfortunately, it's very unlikely that you're good at everything a business requires. If so, I'm damn jealous!

Because no one's good at everything, it's advisable to delegate all tasks to other people that slow you down and hold you back from doing what you're really good at. Your business should make you happy in the long run, and chances are high that accountancy doesn't.

To not just build a business you want to work for, but to be a part of a flourishing community, I'd recommend looking for people in your circle to help you do the jobs that you have no time for or don't have the skillset to take care of it yourself. If you happen to be in a situation where you need to look for people outside of your social environment, you can find many freelancers online.

For this book, I found Ewelina, the illustrator, on Behance, which is a page where graphic designers display their portfolio and you get access to thousands of different styles at an instant. I found Diana, the editor of this book, on Elance, as I was looking for someone who could start working immediately and spoke American English. The designer of this book, who is also named Diana, is someone I went to university with, and while she was in a different department, I always had access to her portfolio as we kept in touch on Facebook.

You can find pages where people offer help with logo design, website design, copywriting, editing, photography, and graphic design, and you can even find virtual assistants to help you with tasks such as booking flights or answering emails. If you are a business that deals with physical goods, you might need help with production.

Here are just a few useful websites to get you started:

www.elance.com
www.odesk.com
www.peopleperhour.com
www.behance.com
www.fiverr.com
www.99designs.com
www.graphicriver.com
www.skillpocket.com

... and there are many more. Just google!

Read the interview with Breanna to learn more about how and why she scaled her business. ◆

187

Breanna Musgrove

ACCESSORIES DESIGNER, VANCOUVER

Before Breanna founded a company, she created a blog to document her adventures in Mexico and her newly discovered passion for dyeing fabrics. Years later, she still runs her business, *Scout & Catalogue*, a company originally inspired by a simple lifestyle by a tropical sea. Breanna discusses here her journey and milestones of her indie business and explains why you shouldn't try to do everything on your own.

What did you study and why?

I have a degree in communication design – I grew up with parents in various creative fields, so design felt like the obvious choice.

What happened between your university diploma and your current career?

After I left school, I worked in an advertising agency and then as the creative director for a woman's retailer. After working for almost a decade, I decided to change things up a bit and I moved to Mexico. I was really inspired by Mexico's artisan culture and began playing with textile dyeing. It was a natural extension to start to sell my goods online and from there, *Scout & Catalogue* was born.

How did you start your business?

Initially, I started a blog and called it *Scout & Catalogue* because I was scouting a new culture and cataloging my experiences. My readers began to express interest in the work I was sharing online and the idea of creating an accessory line came into focus. The handmade movement was just getting started and I was lucky to be one of the first brands out there doing dye work, which made finding a loyal and supportive customer base fairly easy. To this day, I'm very grateful to that online community that first supported me when I lived in a little Mexican house overlooking the Pacific Ocean.

How did you make money in the first couple of months?

I was lucky enough to have a savings account for my time in Mexico, which really took the pressure off of having to make money immediately. The truth is that in most businesses, you just *don't* make money in the first few months because there are always start-up costs to get your idea in action. The important thing is to have a good business plan so that you are aware of how much your initial costs will be, what your projected earnings are, and when you are forecasted to hit your break-even point. Being in business is being comfortable with the constant ebb and flow of investment and return, and planning well can really make the uncertainty a lot more comfortable.

What was your initial investment?

My first big investment was a $ 500 industrial sewing machine which felt like an enormous amount of money at the time. Obviously, I also was paying for material costs – fabrics, leathers and dyes, as well as studio space. I think the biggest and most crucial investment, especially in the first few years, was my time. It takes an enormous amount of time to bring a brand to life, so passion and commitment to your project is imperative.

What would you say were the milestones of your business?

I have moved cities three times in the last five years, so every new location has impacted *Scout & Catalogue* and has resulted in milestone decisions. Living in Mexico, I created my brand out of a sense of play with no real grounding in business reality. From there, I moved to Toronto and worked towards making *S&C* a viable source of income. I came back to Canada in June and didn't make much money from running *Scout & Catalogue* until the Christmas sales in December. I then invested in equipment, hired a studio assistant, and began to expand my social media reach, which in turn increased my customer base.

In Toronto, I continued to experiment with my designs and materials, slowly building a collection that reflected my new surroundings.

When I moved to Vancouver, where I'm currently situated, I took the relocation as an opportunity to streamline my business. I simplified my collection and put the focus back on my first love: textile dyeing. I set up a studio outside of my home and surrounded myself with other creative entrepreneurs that would push and inspire me daily. After five years of doing most of the production myself, I have just made the switch to working with a factory. This is a really exciting development for me and we'll see what adventures unfold for *S&C* with this new partnership.

It was a slow journey, but now, five years later, I feel I'm in a very different place than I was when I first started.

What was a nudging point for you to make radical changes in your business?

Most recently, I had the realization that I couldn't grow a business on my own; I needed to bring in other people to support the change of scale I'm interested in. It was really difficult for me to let go of every aspect of *S&C*, but ultimately I could see that the company's success would only grow if I brought in qualified experts. Accounting, for example, is a weak point for me and, of course, the production expertise of the factory has been a huge asset.

> It takes an enormous amount of time to bring a brand to life, so passion and commitment to your project is imperative.

Every time I made a radical change (an investment in my business) it was always because I was trying to find a way to live a happier life while having a thriving business.

What do you consider the everyday difficulties of running an indie business?

Having a small business is to be constantly running uphill. There are always a million things to do that would have been better done yesterday. It's really hard to carve out time for yourself away from your work, but it's truly crucial. I always forget to do this, but am trying to be better about it.

I already mentioned this in the previous question, but the tendency to want to do everything yourself can really hurt your company. Finding people to help you create your dream will be both a benefit to your business and to your own life balance.

My experience is that my brand is a reflection of me – where I shine, it shines and where I fall, it falls. Finding people that have skills that you don't possess rounds out your business, sets you up to succeed, and gives you the freedom to really push and grow in areas you're passionate about.

How do you market your business?

192

I really credit social media with the success of my business; it all began with a blog and my online community continues to be my largest supporter. Photography is a passion of mine and I love being able to share a behind-the-scenes look of my journey with others. I think people love to see the magic of creating things, especially when they don't create themselves.

Beyond that, I work tirelessly to create the best product I can. I think the best marketing strategy you can have is to over-deliver.

My experience is that my brand is a reflection of me – where I shine, it shines and where I fall, it falls.

Could you give some practical tips to someone who wants to become a professional designer and retailer?

This is an unpopular idea, but my number one tip for someone hoping to get into this business is to work for someone else. I'm so grateful for the time I spent working in the retail industry before going out on my own. Not only do you learn on someone else's dime, but you also make invaluable connections that will only help push your project forward when the time is right.

I would say to stop and make a business plan: hire someone to help you if need be. Starting out smart will only get you to where you want to be faster.

Lastly, don't be paralyzed by perfection. At every turn, do your best, but don't let your (often unrealistic) expectations stop you from getting your idea out into the world. Business is a conversation, so don't be afraid to get talking. ●

○ www.scoutandcatalogue.com
○ instagram.com/scout_catalogue

Move your business out of your bedroom

Ever since the debut of *Sex and the City*, many of us have come to romanticize the idea of working from home, and while it works for some, it definitely doesn't work for others. There are no colleagues in your home to keep you focused, which is why you might end up answering emails while still in bed in the morning and doing laundry in the middle of the day. Some people make it work and can be very productive working in their bedroom, but for others, it's just too easy to get distracted.

There are several possibilities to move your business out of your bedroom: you can rent a desk at a coworking space or at a company you're friendly with. You can work out of a café, or ask a friend who is also a freelancer to work together with you at each other's apartments. If the service *sparechair.me* picks up, chances are high we might soon be able to AirBnB office spaces, which could be really fun!

If you know people who also work on their own just as you do, you can always start a studio space. There are always spaces available for temporary usage, so if you don't want to commit to a space long-term, you can try to find one for a couple of months and try out how it would be to work alongside other people.

The advantage of coworking isn't just the ability to leave work behind once you head home; it's also the community of like-minded people, which you can't have at home. People at coworking spaces usually build a little eco-system, sort of like a collective, and recommend each other to clients.

There are some great coworking spaces around the world: some of them are now chains and as a member, you can rent a desk in one city and visit the other coworking spaces to work from there free of charge for a certain period of time. Some of the more known coworking spaces are *Betahaus*, *ImpactHub*, or *WeWork*. Some of the hidden gems are the *WixLounge* in New York, *Studiomates*, which is also in New York, *Google Campus* in the heart of London, and my absolute favorite, *Seats2Meet*, where you can work free of charge and meet fellow freelancers, thanks to their internal social network. They have spaces in various cities in the Netherlands, Spain, Germany, UK, India, Japan, and Egypt.

If working from home for now is your only option, which doesn't mean I don't prefer to work from home myself, then try to have a space dedicated to work, and work only, to be able to walk away from it and relax once your working hours are over. Buy yourself some fresh flowers, treat yourself to a Skype call with a friend at lunch, or listen to a couple of *Ted.com* talks, as I like to do. Find some other routine that makes you happy and when you feel like you want to see a friendly face, head to a café in your area.

Here is Vicky's story on her career as a fashion blogger and why she decided to stop working from home and rent out an office space instead. ◆

195

Vicky Heiler

FASHION BLOGGER, VIENNA

Vicky started her blog, *Bikinis & Passports*, in 2010 as a travel diary for friends and family. Quickly, however, more and more people started following along and the content changed towards a personal life and style blog. In 2014, her employer moved the department where she worked to another country. Instead of looking for a new job, she took the plunge and started blogging full-time, while also pursuing her second project, *The Daily Dose*. In Vicky's interview, she talks about learning new skills and how she grew her blog into the main source of her income.

What did you study and why?

I studied communication because I always wanted to go into advertising. Only after a couple of internships at various agencies, I figured it wasn't the right fit. Without being a graphic designer or texter, I was stuck in the customer consulting department at the agencies, which was simply not creative enough for me.

What happened between your university diploma and your current career?

I started out with a full-time internship at the digital marketing department of a large fashion retailer. They recruited me because of my blog, which I started writing during my second year of college. I was quickly made responsible for the social media on Facebook and got to partake in strategic decisions and campaigns too. Later on, I cut my hours and only worked part-time for two years because my blog was starting to take up more time.

I always loved my job, but had played with the thought of giving full-time blogging a go for a while. When the company decided to relocate the entire department to Germany, it seemed like the right moment for me to become self-employed.

What made you decide to become a full-time blogger?

I think it's always an easy decision if you get the opportunity to turn a hobby into the main source of your income. At the same time, it's a little intimidating to give up a fixed, monthly paycheck because you never know if it's going to be the same amount of money each month. It made sense to me to become self-employed because I already had a reasonable amount of work experience on my resumé, I was earning money with my blog, and I knew that if this didn't work out, I could always apply for another job. So, in the beginning, I thought I'd just give it a go and if it didn't work out, at least I tried.

How did you manage to turn a side project into the main source of your income?

Whenever your work is something that doesn't feel like work and you enjoy doing it, it's very likely that you're good at it too!

I started blogging in 2010 and it's always been a hobby of mine. After about a year, I was slowly getting small requests, such as writing about a lookbook and getting € 50 for it. It wasn't much, but that was pretty much the start. In 2011, I joined an agency for my blog and that brought me some additional requests. The blog grew slowly and organically, but even at that point, it definitely didn't make enough money for me to be able to live off of it.

In October 2013, I switched agencies and suddenly I was earning more money with my blog than I was in my actual job. I think that's a decent hint that you're doing something right.

> Whenever your work is something that doesn't feel like work and you enjoy doing it, it's very likely that you're good at it too!

I don't think that being a professional blogger is something you can decide and then be a professional blogger the next day: it takes years to grow an audience.

How did you make money in the first couple of months?

In the beginning, the money was more like an allowance. It financed my server costs and camera expenses. I think I only started making regular amounts of money after October 2013 when I switched agencies, so almost four years later!

When I noticed money coming in more regularly, I started keeping lists and comparing it to my "regular" income. After about six months of that, it got to the point where my blog brought in more money than my job. Once I went full-time with the blog, it was like a magical wheel had begun. Things really started falling into place and simultaneously, I was approached by more and more brands. To me, that was a sign that I was heading down the right track!

Something I've learned, and not just because of my situation, but also because of how it was with many of my friends who became self-employed – once you put all your energy into something, it will all start moving.

For example, when I launched *The Daily Dose* together with Kathi Schmalzl, people started approaching us and asking whether we'd like to take care of their social media channels. All these possibilities that came our way would have never been possible if we would have kept our day jobs. You need the time and flexibilities to jump at new opportunities.

How did you find an agency for your blog?
The agency I'm with was recommended to me by another blogger. It's a small agency with only about 25 other blogs. Before, I was with a big agency for years and I wasn't always happy about how they treated me. So when this other agency was recommended to me, I was already half looking for alternatives.

I used to get many suggestions for collaborations that didn't fit my personality and weren't even close to the type of content I like to write about. A big part of being a blogger is sorting through inquiries and deciding what requests are relevant or irrelevant to you. I felt I wasn't being taken care of properly back then.

The agency I'm with now was founded less than two years ago and I can only recommend them because they really know the blogs they represent. They consider you as an individual and treat you accordingly and I really feel like they take a lot of work off my plate.

As a blogger, it's really important to stay true to yourself and your values. Your readers trust you and your taste, and it feels wrong to sell out and present products you wouldn't buy if they weren't sponsored. My current agency is really helpful because they know what brands are good for me. I really enjoy working with them!

How do you choose your clients?

I always consult my agency first. My requirements for the brands I work with on my personal blogs are slightly different than what we demand when featuring brands on *The Daily Dose*.

For my personal blog, I only present brands where I have some kind of a fascination for their story. I don't just post pictures; I have to write a story too, so I really have to be convinced myself.

My main criteria is to work with brands I would personally spend money on: it's the cosmetics I love, fashion brands I admire, or travel destinations I would visit one day.

It's a little different with how Kathi and I see *the Daily Dose*. For *The Daily Dose*, we only work with brands we like, of course, but our clients are a little more diverse, simply because the content is more like that of a magazine and not always quite as personal. For example, we host store openings, write about hotel suggestions, and also include playlists, cocktail recipes, or our personal beauty favorites. The list is long.

There is this romanticized idea of working from home until you find yourself all day by yourself without any social interaction.

How do you organize your work day? Where do you work?

We just got our own office. There is this romanticized idea of working from home until you find yourself all day by yourself without any social interaction. I always enjoyed being around people, getting ready in the morning, and going to the office where I met my colleagues and could chat with them during breaks. I missed that.

My work is my laptop, so technically speaking, I can work from anywhere. However, as soon as I worked from home, I didn't just work from anywhere, but I also worked all the time: I would be cooking dinner and simultaneously responding to my emails.

Getting an office was a big step for us because now, the moment we shut down, our work is over for the day. It really helped me because I can now relax when I get home.

How do you represent yourself online? What platforms do you consider important?

I think that if you have a good sense of humor and are good with words, then Twitter is a great tool. As for me, 140 characters are not enough. I'm a very visual person and I like to write more than Twitter allows. I really like Instagram; it's like an extension of my blog and I can see a lot of people come to my site and click on the link in my Instagram profile. I also use Facebook and Pinterest a lot. I try to always post original content to support my blog.

Could you give some practical tips to someone who wants to become a professional fashion blogger?

First, you must have a message to tell. Be a good writer, a great photographer, have amazing outfits, or draw beautiful illustrations. If you're not good at taking pictures, you should practice because chances are high that you won't succeed if your blog isn't visually appealing. First impressions are really important, so make sure everything looks great for people to stay and come back to see more of what you come up with to entertain and inspire them.

In the beginning when I saw something I liked, I tried to analyze how it's been done. I would search for tutorials on Google until I would find one that taught me the effect I was after. I actually still do that a lot because I read a lot of different blogs myself.

There are so many great tutorials on Youtube to help you learn some background on a certain skill. For example, having an expensive camera and not knowing how to use it is a waste of your money. Switch off the automatic mode and experiment. Learn on the job!

If you want to be successful, you should invest in your blog: not just your time and your drive, but develop a brand, invest in a logo, and get yourself a nice camera.

There are about 70,000 new blogs every day, and if you want to stand out, you really must think of a great concept. And stay true to yourself and your message. Always! ●

○ www.bikinisandpassports.com
○ instagram.com/vickyheiler

203

Work with awesome people

It's very likely that you'll spend more time with people you work with than with your family and friends, which is why you need to be extra careful whom you choose. A business partnership is like a marriage. You must be in zen and completely honest and open with each other. Also, you should always make sure that you have a contract that clarifies your relationship and what happens if things go wrong. No partnership ever starts with bad intentions, but it's possible for a relationship to become sour over time.

In business, there are four types of partnerships and you should have a contract for all of them: your business partners, your investors, your employees or third-party providers, and your customers. Even when you start working with friends, you should have a contract that clarifies the boundaries, expectations, and circumstances if things don't go the way as expected. You should never start working without a contract in your hand because if you sign and didn't see what's expected from you in black and white, you might get disappointed and slowly turn bitter if more things go wrong in a short period of time.

A contract's there to protect both parties, so you're not obliged to blindly accept the terms once a contract is handed to you. Many people don't read through contracts properly and just hand one and the same contract to different people they work with.

In every contract you sign, make sure there is a clear definition of the scope of work. There should also be a clear explanation of what will happen if the project gets cancelled, conditions if the needs of one of the parties change, or terms for if the contractor decides they don't need your services or the work you've produced anymore.

If you're the one supposed to deliver work, make sure the contract states that the unlimited rights to use your work are only enabled once the remuneration has been paid in its full amount.

205 —

Don't be afraid of negotiating because negotiating is what makes a contract fair. I'd recommend to watch the Creative Mornings talk *F*ck you. Pay me!* with Mike Monteiro, and also read the story of Carina and Tanja who founded their business straight out of university.

◆

Tanja Roos &
Carina Schichl

ENTREPRENEURS, MUNICH

Nectar & Pulse is the brainchild of Tanja and Carina who met at university and started their business straight after graduation. Their first product was a personalized travel guide that led to a great number of client requests. They now run a successful design agency out of Munich and focus on high class travel and lifestyle clients. Here, they speak about their business and personal relationships, and how it was for them to start a business without a lot of previous work experience.

What did you study and why?

TANJA: We are both creative minds, so each of us decided to study design and product management at the University in Salzburg and also at the University of the Arts in London.

CARINA: We met during our studies in 2004 and we began collaborating on many projects and really enjoyed working together. We have always been a great team and complement each other well.

What happened between your university diploma and your current career?

TANJA: The concept for *Nectar & Pulse* was my graduation project. After I graduated, I went on a road trip through America and spent six weeks thinking about what I wanted to do with my life. I was scribbling down companies I wanted to work for; *Nectar & Pulse* stayed on the list the longest.

I sent Carina an email and asked her if she was interested to make the project a reality together with me.

CARINA: When the email arrived, I was still working on my own graduation project. I wrote back that she should let me hand in my project first, give me three days to recover, and then I'd be ready!

What were your first steps to realize your business?

CARINA: We locked ourselves in Tanja's nursery at her parents' house where we wrote a business plan. We sold everything, packed our bags, and moved to Stockholm. Tanja is half-Swedish and her family has a cabin in the Swedish woods, so that was where we started.

TANJA: We could live there with quite low costs and without any distractions. We were living like a couple; very isolated from everything and we worked day and night on *Nectar & Pulse*. We started collecting stories from local soulmates, took their pictures, and worked on the design and layout of the travel guide. We had to do a lot of research and it took time to visualize everything. We stayed in Sweden for one and a half years.

During that time, we also found an investor for our business. He is the father of three kids in Great Britain where I worked as an au-pair when I was 16. He was an investment banker for a long time and I have always stayed in touch with him for business questions. We became friends and I consult-

Your business is a reflection of who you are as a person.

ed him when I wrote the diploma thesis to get his point of view on certain aspects. He thought the idea of *Nectar & Pulse* was so powerful and interesting that he suggested becoming a business partner and buy shares. Since the beginning, he's been a great mentor to us.

CARINA: I think it was a good choice because coming straight out of university, our standard of living was already low, so we didn't have to adapt our lifestyle.

TANJA: I think the fact that we were young and naive really made us go for it. We didn't think there were many obstacles, so we were more courageous. We didn't worry too much about consequences and just followed our guts. We didn't even think about the risks. We just did it, worked very hard, and somehow it has all worked out. Of course, with ups and downs.

How did you make money in the first couple of months?

CARINA: We had some savings to live off for a while and we also got some money from selling our possessions.

TANJA: On side, we worked on some design projects, such as designing snowboards or doing a magazine for a friend. Carina also waitressed for a while. In the beginning, we worked seven days a week, day and night. We both looked really tired back then.

CARINA: We didn't just look tired, we were actually exhausted, but we had this big vision of what *Nectar & Pulse* could become and that kept us going.

TANJA: In the beginning, we really didn't have a balanced life. We worked 24/7; if not in front of the computers, then in our heads. *Nectar & Pulse* was constantly on our minds.

How long did it take you to be able to live off your business?

TANJA: It must have been about three and a half years.

CARINA: We made money, just not any profits. It took us about one and a half years until we had the first few sales and then it grew slowly but steadily from there. When we started, we sold our guides in selected shops and through our online store. The online sales were always stronger, so we decided to focus more on that.

TANJA: Because we have a product, we had to invest a lot in the beginning: we bought 4,000 ring binders, paper, and also the printing costs were quite significant.

CARINA: We had to get proper equipment, such as a good camera to be able to shoot proper pictures, and having our website appear the way we wanted it to look also cost quite a lot of money.

You first had a product before you moved into consulting. Can you describe how it happened?

CARINA: We were focused on marketing our products and developing additional travel guides when the Austrian Tourism Board approached us. They were looking for someone who would help them make a book about the best designers and architects in the regional capitals of Austria.

TANJA: Most clients found us because they had one of our travel guides or stumbled upon our website and then asked if we would be interested in producing content and photos for their media. It was great to see that we could provide more value to brands.

CARINA: And one day in 2013, BMW knocked on our door and asked us to organize an inspiration trip for a design research project. That was our first big client.

TANJA: From then on, one thing led to another. The big clients mainly want our branding and trend know-how, design skills, and network of inspiring influence-makers around the globe.

How do you represent yourself online? What platforms do you use?

CARINA: We have a website and we're now working on a relaunch. We use Facebook, Instagram for *Nectar & Pulse*, and then we also have our own Instagram accounts.

TANJA: When we first started, we had a blog to document our start-up journey. We made a bunch of videos and I think it was fun for people to follow. We discontinued the website when we didn't have anymore time to publish content on it because there were so many other projects that kept us busy.

Now, every time we hire an intern, we show them our small startup documentary for them to better understand the brand. I think every entrepreneur should keep a diary of their progress. It helps to exchange with like-minded others who are going through the same phase in their lives.

Interesting people are everywhere and you never know which meeting leads to a future project.

How do you meet your clients?

CARINA: We go to a lot of parties, fashion and travel fairs, conferences, and shop and gallery openings. I think it's important to interact with people, not just online but also offline.

TANJA: You can never plan meetings: when we were standing in the queue to board our plane to Marrakech, we met Steve-O from Jackass. Interesting people are basically everywhere and you never know which meeting leads to a future project.

What would you recommend to someone who wants to turn their idea into a viable business?

CARINA: You'll need a lot of commitment and ideas for projects you're really passionate about.

TANJA: And you'll also need people around you to remind you why you started. When things get tough, it's good to be surrounded by people who believe in you and remind you of your vision. It's a lot of trial and error and you have to allow yourself to make mistakes, reflect on what went wrong, and fix it. That's a big part of being responsible for your own income. I think that it's all part of personal growth and your business is a reflection of who you are as a person. So the way you grow, your business grows, and vice versa. Always keep the big picture in mind. What difference do you want to make as a human and with your business for the world?

CARINA: And not to forget, even if you have a lot of work on your plate, don't forget to have fun!

211 —

What would you recommend to someone who wants to start a business with their friend?

TANJA: If you both already think about it, you should definitely do it because you'll spend a lot of time together, so it's crucial you spend all that time with someone you really like.

CARINA: You must remain very clear and have open communication to discuss everything. Being business partners is like being married because, especially in the beginning, you spend so much time together and have to deal with all the ups and downs. Always be honest with each other and agree on each other's conditions, even if it's uncomfortable at times. ●

○ www.nectarandpulse.com
○ instagram.com/nectarandpulse

Have a side project

Now, as we're approaching the end of this book, you must have recognized that many of the careers described in the interviews started off as side projects. Not everyone has the budget to build a business and fully focus on building it from day one.

Maybe you can't start your big, freelancer career tomorrow, but you can start building your freelance career a little bit every day. If having a successful business of your own is your dream, then that's a big dream. You can't expect to be able to take one big step today and achieve your dream tomorrow; you have to make several small steps to reach what you aspire to be. The question is, when are you going to take the first small step?

Start small: get up a little earlier tomorrow and do a little bit of something you're passionate about every day from now on.

Get into the habit of creating and pursuing a side project. Treat your side project as a labor of love and build it slowly so that one day, you'll be able to leave your day job behind and focus on your side project fully.

You can start doing just about anything and you can even learn new skills and develop something from scratch. Some people started making a magazine, others started a blog, others spent ten hours a week working on their Instagram feed; it doesn't matter what you enjoy and what you want to be doing, and it doesn't even matter if this should be a business one day or not.

All that matters is that you enjoy yourself.

Get ready to be impressed by Victoria's incredible story on how she started her magazine while still in high school and what her plans are once she graduates from university. ◆

Victoria Jin

MAGAZINE EDITOR, BEIJING

It doesn't matter how old you are or what your current situation is, it's never too late, or too early, to start building your future.

Victoria is still a student, but one that runs a magazine with more than 200,000 views. While she keeps KNEON as her side project to still focus on graduating, she knows that she will soon be able to take the right steps to turn KNEON, the magazine she founded when she was 17, into a viable business. In her truly stellar story, she shares how it all started and how KNEON organically gained traction.

What did you study and why?

Actually, I haven't graduated yet. I study art history and Chinese studies. Originally, I wanted to study fine art, but my parents were worried that I might not be able to make a living as an artist, so I decided to focus on the academic side of the arts.

How did you come up with the concept for KNEON, your magazine?

When I was 17, I had my own fashion blog and mostly posted my outfits, but every time one of my friends found my blog, I always felt slightly embarrassed. I had to come up with something where my appearance or 'body' wasn't the sole product.

I wanted to create a project that would allow me to meet more interesting people, to allow for more collaboration and sharing of ideas. I never thought the project would be still alive after all these years and I definitely didn't think it could eventually become a business.

After KNEON existed for about three years, people started getting interested in the magazine and its potential. I've had the magazine for more than five years, and I think that if I would now decide to focus on it full-time, I could make a living out of it.

How does KNEON work from the financial perspective?

After about two years, I ran into someone who worked at Levi's. They had a spare budget and he casually mentioned that they were buying media space and we could agree on an advertising partnership. I was really excited that someone was interested in KNEON enough to want to purchase advertising. This was the first time I felt like the magazine was validated as a 'business.'

KNEON is an online magazine, so the only fixed costs we have are the € 50 we spend on our website and emails once a year. Everything else we earn, we invest back into the business to print business cards or posters, or take part in pop-ups to help further promote.

We're just a small group of people who work on the magazine, and we're all still at university. It's becoming increasingly harder to balance school and the magazine, but I just don't have the time to invest in truly developing the magazine, and my dream, to make it into print.

Our whole team works together and we all reach out to advertisers for each issue by calling and emailing people to ask them if they'd like to buy ad space in the magazine.

I'm really proud that everyone who works on KNEON or contributes to it does it free of charge just because they care about the project. I believe that I really managed to prove that you can produce editorials and great content that is easy-on-the-eyes without having a team of 10 or 15 people on set.

I want to keep everything as it is until I graduate and then I will try to develop the magazine. I want to hire a graphic designer, a developer, and definitely someone for business development.

I'm glad I started on my own because it gave me the opportunity to really get to know the product, find a voice, and specify a style and a direction.

How much time do you usually spend working on KNEON?
Everyday, I dedicate about three to four hours to KNEON, so it's probably about 100 hours every month.

What were your first steps to publish the first issue?
I started with choosing a name. I still think it's really important to have a good name and a good branding. I had a few name options and wasn't sure which one was the best, so I opened a poll and asked my blog readers. They liked the name KNEON the most.

The first issue I made was mainly for my blog readers. I was directly involved in most of the content; the interviews, commissioning of illustrations, editing articles, and photographing, but I did reach out to a couple of photographers I knew in Vienna and asked them if they'd like to contribute. Also at that time, I was doing test-shoots for a modeling agency in Vienna, so I included photos I shot for them too. I interviewed some bloggers and reached out to illustrators who liked the idea and provided their work. Everyone was really excited and helped out with the content. When I think back, what mattered most was that I felt comfortable reaching out to all these different people. I enjoyed creating content with others to form a single idea. 217

I didn't mean for KNEON to become a business or a 'legit' magazine, for lack of a better word, so I didn't feel much pressure for it to be on par with professional magazines right away. It was kind of self-indulging; the content just really had to please my vision.

I am glad I started the magazine on my own because it gave me the opportunity to really get to know the product, find a voice, and specify a style and a direction.

Looking back, the first issue was very basic and it was mainly image-based. Only later on did we start adding interviews, more articles, and featured content. I think it took me about two months to finalize the first issue of KNEON, and now we release a new issue each season (four times a year).

What would you say were your steps to establish KNEON as the magazine it is today?
I think the one breakthrough that helped us a lot was utterly unintentional at that time: I really loved to go to concerts and *The Shout Out Louds* were coming to the city. I didn't have tickets, so there was no way for me to go. But then, because I didn't have anything to lose, I emailed their PR agent and said, 'Hi, I'm Victoria from KNEON and

I would like to interview the band.' They replied and invited me. That was a big moment!

Having *The Shout Out Louds* in my portfolio helped immensely, and I included a link to their feature for the next time. From there, the list grew organically. A couple of months later, it wasn't just me reaching out to PR agencies anymore, but PR agencies were pitching to me to interview their clients. In 2012, the PR agency of *Tomorrowland* asked if I would be interested in covering the 3-day festival in Belgium. At the time, I didn't know how big it was, but I agreed. It was through that opportunity that I got to interview some of the greatest DJs in the world, which was also a milestone for KNEON, as it meant we were being taken seriously.

That helped shape the profile of KNEON enormously because I was no longer just producing a photography magazine, but one with interesting interviews and portraits of people who were known for their art and craft. The magazine and its readership numbers have grown steadily over the years.

How do you market the magazine?

We don't pay for any advertising, send out newsletters, or work with a PR agency. I think the fact that we have so many people who regularly contribute to the magazine and then share it with their friends and followers across social media is a major help. We get about 200,000 to 300,000 unique readers per issue.

Do your research: see what already exists in the area you want to dive into and work on a concept that stands out.

How do you represent yourself online?

I only really use Instagram. I'm still trying to revive my blog because once you start posting irregularly, people drop out and look for regular, fun content somewhere else. But apart from those two mediums, and the odd tweet every now and then, I'm quite an anxious person when it comes to online self-representation.

I think it's important to have a face for every project you do because then people don't just follow the product, but they follow the person behind it and it allows you as the creator to do different things and grow an audience. Elin Kling is a perfect example: she's established herself as a brand with a specific creative direction, so any future ventures she decides to embark on, she will always have a following and a fanbase.

What has been especially challenging for you in the last five years while running KNEON?

One of the biggest challenges has been to find the right team. I'm not in a position at the moment to offer salaries to my team members, so it's mainly friends and people throughout my university who help me with the editorial and development. I experienced that it can get a little uncomfortable if you're working with a close friend and they fail to deliver to your expectations. I felt uncomfortable reminding them of deadlines – after all, they were doing it voluntarily.

When it comes to hiring for a startup, I think the most important thing is to select carefully and see what they can offer that you can't do yourself. It's the only way a small team can create the biggest impact.

Could you give some practical tips to someone who wants to start a magazine?

Before you start anything, get to know your neighbors. Do your research: see what already exists in the area you want to dive into and work on a concept that stands out. Find that cozy niche for your magazine. Also, make sure that there is interest. There is no point starting a magazine on a topic that doesn't have much potential readership.

I also highly advise not to hire a big team right away. Start with a partner or two team members at most. One other person who has different skills than you is enough. You don't want to feel too much pressure to get it right immediately. You will need time to work on the concept on your own, to see what works and what doesn't. Your magazine will be much more nimble than if you had a big team that really looked to you to get it accurate right off the bat.

Really work to make the magazine your own: find your voice, decide on your logo, your visual and writing style, and be consistent. Use the same logo and the same style of visuals across all channels to not confuse your followers, who will remain loyal as long as you maintain the quality and novelty of your content.

Lastly, be aware of deadlines. It's incredibly important to stick to your own release dates (I learned the hard way). People will email you and ask what happened and why your magazine isn't online yet, so always stay on top of your game. ●

○ www.ellevictoire.com
○ instagram.com/ellevictoire

Don't accept "no" for an answer

Do you sometimes feel you're stuck and there is no way out? Do you crave more time off to do what you're really passionate about? Do you have dreams of how you want to live and what you want to be doing?

It often seems that our dreams are dependent on other people's decisions, and as it usually goes, the people who could give us our dream opportunity just don't.

So, what happens if that particular person who could doesn't give you the break you want so badly? Does it mean you should give up on your dream?

Of course not!

If someone else doesn't give you the chance you think you deserve, then you must either find the person who will or create the opportunity yourself:

If you want to be a museum curator, then start curating without the museum;

If you want to be a magazine editor, then it's your time to self-publish a magazine on Issuu;

If you want to be a singer, you have to get out there and sing.

Nowadays, you can have almost any career on a freelance basis, and with the use of social media, you can also market it yourself. Don't accept "no" for an answer from people who are trying to discourage you. It's all in your hands, and you need to manifest your own happiness.

The time has come to present you with the last interview with Tina: you can learn a lot from her persistence, dedication, and drive to achieve her dreams. ◆

Tina Toplak

SINGER-SONGWRITER, LONDON

"Only try to become a singer if there is nothing else that would make you happy." For 24 years, Tina tried to find a profession that would make her happy, but wasn't very successful. She didn't want to waste anymore time looking and instead, decided to take the leap and follow her calling.

Tina's persistency, hard work, and realization of not wanting to do anything but become a singer-songwriter helped her stay on track. In this final interview, Tina speaks about the different ways to make money as a musician and also explains the importance of industry contacts to eventually become successful.

225

What did you study and why?

I've always loved singing and wanted to become a singer ever since I was a little girl. My family wanted to make sure I had an education that would eventually pay my rent, so I studied media management.

What happened after you graduated?

After graduation, I decided to get another degree and study music performance. I moved to London to be in a city where there is a proper music scene to broaden my chances of becoming an artist. I was finally studying what I was passionate about, but after a while, I felt like the course was killing my creativity, which is why I eventually decided to quit.

What made you decide to become a singer?

I didn't want to become a singer; I wanted to become a singer-songwriter. As a session singer, you are seen as a session musician for commercial gigs or as a background vocalist, which isn't a bad way to earn money, but it wasn't the path I wanted to take.

I've always wanted to become an artist and write my own songs and play piano, but first I had to go through the experience of not wanting to become a session singer.

When I was at university, a big part of what I learned was to cover other artists. No support was offered if someone wanted to interpret songs creatively. It wasn't the right choice for me and it felt like a waste of my time and energy. So, even though I currently earn money as a session musician, I really put all my energy into making my career as an artist work.

What were your steps to become a singer?

I've always been singing, writing, and playing piano from a very young age, and I've been in a couple of small concerts too.

In London, I started building my network: I talked to my teachers and asked them for industry contacts. I went to different producers, which often turned out to be a horrifying experience. People in this industry often are dodgy, which you only notice when their 'so-called studio' isn't really a studio, but more like a bedroom with a computer and two speakers.

All these stories you might have heard about the scene unfortunately aren't just stories. There are hundreds of girls out there trying to 'make it,' which is the perfect opportunity for perverts and criminals. So, one of the main challenges is to find the right people to work with. It takes time to develop valuable relationships.

The other challenge is to find good locations where you can perform. With singing, it's all word-of-mouth, so you really have to find a location where your voice sounds great for people to tell their friends about the amazing performance they heard the other night.

Often, good locations make you either pay or ask you to bring 15 friends who all have to pay the entry fee and their drinks, and note that you won't get any money for these gigs either. It's different in every country, but you should be aware of the fact that many singers must pay to sing at a venue.

How did you make money in the first couple of months?

In the beginning, I lived off my student loan. I started to look for jobs that were at least industry related. I'm part of about ten agencies and I often get jobs through people I know.

I've done a lot of modeling, acting work, or sometimes, I've even worked as a hostess or waitress. I also work with a cover band and soon I'm going to start teaching, which will take off some of the financial pressure. It's a portfolio of little jobs that allow me to focus on what I eventually want to do with my life.

What's the best way for a singer to make money?

As a session musician, it's most likely that you will earn your income with music. There are agencies that specialize in representing session musicians and also agencies that represent background vocalists. Session vocalists provide voice-overs, back-up vocals, studio vocals, commercials, trailers, and so on.

There is a wide range of jobs you can do as a session musician, but you need to be on top of your game and have good agencies and contacts because there are so many people who do the same job. I believe that it's a way into the industry – not a very glamourous one – but everyone has to start somewhere. Many musicians also make money with teaching.

If you really want to become a singer-songwriter, then you must be extremely persistent and find your own way, which I think is the hardest part of becoming a singer. Find a niche, find you, and find something no one else can offer.

It takes time to develop valuable relationships.

I've done some research on how successful people became successful and when I connect the dots, it seems that the one thing they all have in common is their dedication and that becoming successful was the only thing they wanted.

How did you find your producer?

I was recommended to him by my former bass player. My now-producer came to my concert and that's how he decided he wanted to work with me. He has a home studio and works privately, so not with a big company, but he has already worked with some big names and companies too and is good at what he does. I don't have to sell my whole life to work with him.

What social media channels do you use and what platforms do you consider important?

First, I think that it's important to have business cards on you at all times, so when you talk to people and then they look for you online, they have immediate access to your music.

You really must put yourself out there and have a good Facebook and Instagram account. The bigger your audience, the better. You need to be active on Youtube, Reverbnation, and Soundcloud. Additionally, I use Bandmix.com and DittoMusic.com, which are platforms dedicated to musicians and real music nerds.

Getting all of this content together and posting regularly isn't easy because I'm a one woman business! In my industry when you're starting out, you do everything yourself and because everyone in the industry is really busy, you can't rely on other people to help you.

How do you market yourself and your music?

It's a very long process. First, you must figure out who you are, what you stand for, and create a persona.

You have to know what you sing about; what values you communicate. You should also build a brand for yourself before you start marketing yourself. I already think about how I will sell myself while I make music. I

> I already think about how I will sell myself while I make music. I don't think I do it perfectly, but I'm improving every day.

don't think I do it perfectly, but I'm improving every day.

I'm also going to networking events, which London offers a lot, and there I'm trying to talk to as many people as possible. I'm currently looking for a label, which is why I've recently finished working on my EP. Next, I plan on sending it to everyone I know, so more people who don't know me (yet) will get to hear my music.

What tips would you give to someone who wants to become a professional singer?

Only do it if there is no other profession that would make you happy. I feel that more than in any other industry, you are dependent on other people. The industry is going to break you if you don't know who you are and what you want, so you really have to build a thick skin and live for your goal.

Practice, every day, as much as you can. There are so many people whose voice and appearance are smashing and you have to distinguish yourself from everyone else, so find your voice, work on your online presence, and talk to as many people as possible. Don't accept 'no' for an answer! ●

229 ———

○ www.tina-toplak.com
○ twitter.com/tinatoplakmusic

Think globally

Thank you so much for reading this book to the very last chapter! I hope the interviews have inspired you as much as they have inspired the team that worked on this book together.

The women interviewed for this book are not from one location, but rather they are from different cultures and live in different countries. All of them face different governmental and social circumstances, which is why this book gives no specific information on how to start a business in your country.

The one thing all of these women have in common, however, is that they use the social web to market their services and are confident about what they do to promote it. The internet has given us a tool we can all use to showcase our talents and find customers, co-workers, and collaborators.

No longer do we need to be in one place, sitting at one and the same table to work as a team. No longer do we need to produce work people will buy exclusively in the area where we live. And no longer does it matter where we are geographically to have the careers we want to have.

A couple of months ago, I read *Founders at Work* by Jessica Livingston and felt a little envious of the people who could start their businesses in the early nineties: the internet was so new and fresh and it felt like you could do anything you wanted. A couple of months later, I realized how now is really the time that we can have the careers we want and live where we want, which doesn't have to be one of the hot spots where everything is supposedly happening. I'm saying this because when I was a little girl growing up in a rural village, I felt a little hopeless from time to time because it felt like there were no real opportunities. Now, with the internet, this thought just seems so obsolete to me because truly, it no longer matters where I'm spending my days to work with the people I like. The only thing that matters is what I want to work on, which is something I hope you can establish for yourself.

The team that worked on this book is spread across two continents: the illustrator, Ewelina Dymek, calls Poznań in Poland her home; Diana Ovezea, the responsible art director of *This Year Will Be Different*, lives in The Hague in the Netherlands; and Diana Joiner, who edited the book, works out of Maryland in the US. This book was written in several cafés in London and finalized at my home-office in Vienna.

I found the girls on various social networks where they displayed their work and their skills. Apart from Diana, the art director, I have not yet met the other girls in person, but I hope to do so in the future.

We used Dropbox, Google Docs, Email, and Skype to organize our work flow and to keep up-to-date on everyone's progress.

231

> Now, with the internet, it no longer matters where I'm spending my days to work with the people I like. The only thing that matters is what I want to work on, which is something I hope you can establish for yourself.

The idea of this book came to me one early morning after waking up, and it took about two and a half months to realize it. It was a dream I have had for years, and I'm truly happy you were a part of making it a success.

If you have any questions or just want to say hi, please email to monikanokova@gmail.com.

Also, please send your friends to *thisyearwillbedifferent.com*, share an image of the book on Instagram, and mention the book with #thisyearwillbedifferent on Twitter or Facebook. We hope you found this book helpful and will give it to your BFF for their birthday or whenever you decide they need some inspiration to take the next step in their lives.

On behalf of the team, I hope your year will be different and much better than the last one.

232

Love,
Monika, Diana, Ewe, and Diana Jean ◆

233

Monika Kanokova

Monika Kanokova gave up long ago on trying to define one single location as her home as much as she has given up on trying to find a job title that would summarize what she does. She has a fascination for city building and space design and its impact on people's lives. Her interest in social mobility has planted her interest in people's stories and their unique career paths. She specializes in technology-based communication solutions for them to have positive impacts on people's relationships.

Legally, she's a freelance advertiser, but as she doesn't believe in classic advertising, her design driven approach often leads to unconventional solutions.

She helps her clients with building useful products, optimising customer relationships and communication by adding value to people's lives. If you're wondering how you could improve the communication with your customers or local communities, don't hesitate to contact her.

Web	www.mkanokova.com
Twitter	@mkanokova
Email	monikanokova@gmail.com

Diana Joiner

Diana Joiner always knew she wanted to become an editor and writer one day, although she graduated with an English degree with a specialty in secondary education. After she graduated, she left her home country of the US for the first time to spend the next seven months living, working, and traveling in Thailand. While teaching English abroad, she rediscovered her passions and knew when she returned to the US, she would do things a bit differently than expected.

Now, Diana is pursuing her dreams, and debuted with this very project, *This Year Will Be Different*, as a freelance proofreader and copy-editor. She's dedicated to helping writers effectively deliver their message, while collaborating with them to revise, edit, and polish their work. She's confident that more opportunities lie ahead, and she realizes she will make those opportunities happen. If you're a writer with an inspiring and relatable message, or have a unique and creative story to tell, Diana's writing skills and imagination will help you deliver.

Web   www.dianajoiner.com
Twitter @JoinerEdits
Email   djjoiner925@gmail.com

Diana Ovezea

Diana Ovezea is a growing graphic and type designer who embraces being an "international." She spent her childhood in Romania, where she learned to play in the dirt, chase chickens, and not take things for granted. She spent most of her school years in Austria (while attending the American International School of Vienna), which taught her about tolerance, languages, and embracing the arts. After completing a master course in type design at the Royal Academy of Arts in The Hague, she stayed in The Netherlands.

Diana enjoys working on complex typographic projects, such as designing infographics, books, identities, and custom fonts. She makes an effort to create structure and meaning in her client's projects because she believes that synthesizing, analyzing, and optimizing are important aspects of design. If your company wants to differentiate itself through a custom font, logo, or entire branding; if you need to design a book or a magazine; or if you need a hand-crafted wedding invitation, Diana's expertise will help you achieve the desired visual impact. She only has one requirement for any client or colleague: passion.

Web   www.ovezea.com
Twitter @typemuseum
Email   type.design@me.com

Ewelina Dymek

Ewelina Dymek is a self-taught illustrator who lives in Poznań, Poland. Although she graduated with a diploma in English studies, she decided to follow her greatest passion, which is drawing, and therefore became a freelance illustrator. After graduation, she began another degree in graphic design, which turned out to be extremely handy in illustrating, as Ewelina combines both traditional and digital media in her work.

Apart from drawing and design, Ewelina's also interested in fashion. A few years ago, she discovered a way to combine these hobbies, thus becoming familiar with fashion illustration, for which she uses her imagination to interpret a particular designer's collection and work on fashion brands' campaigns. Ewelina has always wanted to be a fashion illustrator, but with more commissions coming in from various companies not always related to fashion, she discovered how exciting it is to explore her horizons and work with creative people outside the fashion industry. She's always ready to face new drawing challenges and gain new experiences.

Web   www.behance.net/edmk
Twitter @ewelinadmk
Email   ewelinadmk@gmail.com

Meet the Kickstarter backers

We were successfully funded on Kickstarter to get the first edition of *This Year Will Be Different* printed.

We asked our backers to share their contact details. If you're looking for someone to help realize your project, reach out to someone in our community.

Coaching

Andrea L. Messina	www.thisinspiredlife.net
Bettina Sturm	www.deincopilot.de
Dominique Caspers	www.souldrivenlife.com
Tiffany Rowe	www.stillpointstrategies.com

Communications

Alexandra Prasch	www.contentessa.at
Amanda Dean	www.thedreamofawriter.wordpress.com
Claudia Apel	www.claudialovesfashion.com
Julia Basagic	www.fanfarella.at
Kathrin Folkendt	www.kathrinfolkendt.com
Klaus Heller	www.klausheller.at
Macy Lao	macylao.tumblr.com
Michael Jones	de.linkedin.com/in/michaelbjones
Michelle Lee	www.michellelee.is/online
Nadine Knobelsdorf	www.style-taxi.com

Patrick Gevas	www.patrickgevas.com
Patrick Langwallner	www.patresinger.com
Steve Finan	www.facebook.com/finan

Design

Colin Willox	www.colinwillox.com
Felipe Tofani	www.ftofani.com
Gabriel X.	www.gabrielx.com
Josh Tregenza	www.joshtregenza.com
Jürgen D. Hassler	www.twitter.com/juergenhassler
Kyle Studstill	www.alwayscomposure.com
Mauro Rego	www.maurorego.com
Nik Baerten	www.pantopicon.be

239 ——

Development

André Kishimoto	www.kishimoto.com.br
Mart Anthony	www.about.me/martanthony

Engineering

Bastian Eggers	www.twitter.com/espressomaniac
Christian Lendl	www.christianlendl.com
Malia Gonzales	www.livereaddiscover.wordpress.cvom

Entrepreneurs

Florian Hackenberger	www.hackenberger.at
Melissa Aho	www.melissaaho.com
Peter Buchroithner	www.buchroithner.com
Sissel Hansen	www.startupguide.world

Illustration

Eugene To	www.eugeneto.com
Grace Teoh	www.gracify.co
Katherine Reynolds	www.facebook.com/KatkarArtandCraft

Languages

Irene Maria Dias Valente	www.facebook.com/TranslationIsMyWorld
Michael Schmitz	www.smartergerman.com

Photography

Caryn Darlington	www.timeinglass.com
Cliff Kapatais	www.pixelcoma.at
Lukas Havranek	www.in-the-street.com
Niko Zuparic	www.zuparino.com
Tony Gigov	www.tonygigov.com

Product Design

Jonno Riekwel	www.polyon.co
Sarper Erel	www.sarper.se

Research

Dr. Volker Göbbels	www.technologyscout.de
Vanessa Cobb	www.atass.com

Storytelling

Franziska Schmid	www.veggie-love.de
Jacqueline Berman	www.urbane-nomad.com
Yitka Winn	www.yitkawinn.com

Strategy

Justin McMurray	www.juzmcmuz.com
Marah Köberle	www.koeberle.me
Richard Hemmer	www.hemmer.co
Sarah Kickinger	www.ravenandfinch.com
Steffen Stäuber	www.createmeaning.com

Other incredible services

Andreas Grois	www.grois.info
Antares Reisky	www.adviseplus.de
Ashley May Oppon	www.dreadlocktarot.com
Axel Jan Gros	www.xl-g.de
Bec Mutch	www.thecoworkco.com
Emery Hurst Mikel	www.creativelyhealing.com
Jeska Dzwigalski Kittenbrink	www.geekswithdrinks.com
Kathryn Nicole DiMenichi	www.thirdstreetgoods.com
Keith Earl Weber II	www.starlighttea.com

Lawrence Maskill   www.dragonhorsesky.com
Sophie Holzapfel-Epstein   www.swarina.com
Tracy Ann Essoglou, PhD   www.taeartwork.com

The printing of the first edition of this book was also supported by
Annique Senten, Ari Scarlett, Ben Hudson, Casey Condon, Chloé
Lefebvre Fortin, Chris T. Vrem, Clemens Purrucker, Derek Duff,
Dominique Hamilton, Elizabeth M. Johnson, Francis Mallet, Freda Eang,
James Foster, Jeffrey Campbell, Jessica Orr, Joelle Prokupek, Joshua
Marcus-Black, Karin Zölzer, Kayla Halleur, Kelly Beckwith, Kevin Masse,
Kevin Reiterer, Kimberly A. Gandy, Leslie Barkley, Madalyn Pettenati,
Severine Brichard-Rooney and 282 other incredible people.
Thank you!

241 ——

◆

23932416R00143

Printed in Poland
by Amazon Fulfillment
Poland Sp. z o.o., Wrocław